CRY HOPE

Positive Affirmations
For Healthy Living

Jan Veltman

Health Communications, Inc.
Deerfield Beach, Florida

Library of Congress Cataloging-in-Publication Data

Veltman, Jan
    Cry Hope: positive affirmations for healthy living
      by Jan Veltman.
      p.   cm.
    ISBN 0-932194-74-5
    1. Self-perception. 2. Self-actualization (Psychology).
3. Peace of mind. 4. Mental suggestion. 5. Hope. I. Title.
II. Title: Affirmations for healthy living.
BF697.5.S43V44 1988   88-7193
155.2 — dc19   CIP

© 1988 Jan Veltman

ISBN 0-932194-74-5

Published by: Health Communications, Inc.
                Enterprise Center
                3201 S.W. 15th Street
                Deerfield Beach, FL 33442

DEDICATION

This book is dedicated to my grandchild, Brittney, and to our beloved planet Earth, in the hope that love pulls us through and that we never give up.

ACKNOWLEDGMENTS

I wish to thank my parents and my daughters for loving me no matter what; my friends for teaching me so beautifully about living; and most of all, my husband, Johnny, for sharing the Vision and for always encouraging.

Life is always a daring adventure.

Each cell bursts with joy
Every second
You are born.

FOREWORD

This is a book about hope and constructive action. It is a book meant to sing out optimistically amid the worldly clamor and many words of doom. It is a guide to life transformation; and it is important — for truly the creation of a loving, joyful life in union with the Higher Self is the greatest of all works.

Calls to Courage, Cries of Hope

Under a relentless moon
She cried
   shouts of despair
   whimpers of pain
Remorse bitter on her tongue.
Rage rattled swords among her ribs.

Purged then
   in clarity moon-flooded
The cries were calls
Calls to courage
Calls to healing
Calls to drown the battle sounds
Cries of trust
   of resurrection
   of yearning, yeasting
      yielding
Cries to summon life
Cries of Hope.

INTRODUCTION

Every thought is a sorcerer. The subconscious is immensely powerful and language is vital in programming that vast mind beyond ordinary awareness. We are reminded of ancient wisdom in the origin of the word "spell." Words are magic. Languaging is a wondrous, creative gift.

Sitting in the mire of repeated depression, I had one thing going for me — I love words. I have always believed in the magic of words to entertain, to persuade, to teach, to express and ventilate. After a lifetime of negative thinking, of worrying, of paralyzing fear, some kind soul lifted the corner of my dark blanket and shed a radiant beam of light — the idea of "affirmations." I was ready to work some of the magic on myself.

I remember the first affirmation I tried, repeating it to myself once every hour. It went something like, "I am deserving of the best the universe has to offer." Rebellious feelings arose at first. My "poor me" identity was threatened. But some deep, inner wisdom perked up its sweet ears and kept listening, insisting that I pay attention. After the repetitions became rote, after little notes (written by my Wise Self) appeared daily under the toothpaste and on the refrigerator, something clicked. I began at some sacred moment to believe it.

The effects were subtle. I think I stood taller and made more phone calls. Some of those contacts paid off. I don't recall having consciously decided to take action, yet suddenly I was moving in a positive direction, feeling better and wondering where the energy was coming from.

My Wise Self knew. I continued to create affirmations that felt good to me. I gathered words of courage from many sources. I read everything I could find on programming the subconscious.

A favorite affirmation was, "I am opening emotional space for feeling good." During deep breathing, I exhaled it. At lunch, I chewed and swallowed it with the first five bites. Before sleep, it was a prayer, full of gratitude and hope.

Still, external conditions changed slowly or not at all. I fell back and was tempted to throw away the golden words. But I had felt the power and continued the system of positive reprogramming.

Affirming the good often seemed inadequate among a legion of old habits. Every negative thought sent vibrations through my whole being and beyond, creating a more negative reality. A spoiled child inside obviously got some pay-off for "gritching and moaning" and for "awfulizing." That spoiled child was part of me and was firmly entrenched. I resented having to spend time and energy changing it, but this had to stop.

And "Stop!" eventually became the command to break the negative cycle. Early in the "garbage out" campaign, however, I could only witness myself playing "ain't it awful" and "poor-no-good-me." I would watch myself kick me for doing it. A step in the right direction was to quit kicking me for kicking me. I began to simply observe and say inwardly, "There it is again. Hmmm . . ." The hurting child inside was perceived as a more valuable part of myself, a part that kept me from nodding off into complacency, a part that needed healing and new skills.

I could honestly begin to say, "I am loving every part of myself and so I grow."

From the more benign witness position it was a short but crucial step to the "Stop!" technique. It became a gratifying chase, "catching" negative self-talk and facing it down with, "Stop! This is not productive."

Replacing the old automatic thoughts was also a challenge. Initially, deep breathing granted a little mental/emotional space and a general, prememorized affirmation filled it in.

The natural course of evolution in this process led me to create affirmations that would more thoroughly replace the "trash" thoughts I was continually detecting. Global generic affirmations begged to be joined with many that were more specific. Almost every affirmation in this book is the flip-side, then, of a once-negative piece of mental software. I simply wrote a whole new set of programs.

My subconscious has heard those instructions, upgrading all systems. Physical problems have cleared up or greatly improved. Beautiful relationships are growing out of a basic good attitude and healthier self-esteem. A deep emotional stability and inner peace are the greatest gifts.

The process continues, for it takes a lifetime to become the most wonderful self possible. It takes a lifetime of moment-to-moment decisions to choose joy, to build our own purposeful and invigorating perceptions.

I am grateful to all of those who came before, offering the choice of affirmation, and to all those heroic people in my life whose rebirth testifies to the power of those choices. They remind me over and over. When I forget and slide back, one affirmation returns me to the path, "I remember now my choice to lift and heal with my thoughts, beginning with myself."

Part of your choice is reflected in your reading this book, daily focusing on the hope and the blessings. Creating your own affirmations is even more empowering. We build our psychic muscle every time we accept the challenge, stepping in and taking over the inner air waves.

For me, it is like solving riddles. What belief or thought is creating this feeling? It all seems lighter now, like a game — any negative thought is a piece to be played. There are no losers in this game. We can all win.

To give you an idea of how the process works and of the metamorphosis that occurs, some examples follow:

1. *Initial negative thought* (grist for the mill): "Look at all she's accomplished. I'm nothing compared to her."

Inner voice: "There I go again. Stop! This is not productive." (3 deep breaths) "Now, what can I make out of this that will help me?"

Affirmations:
"I will allow only interest and positive motivation when I notice differences between myself and others. Every person's situation is unique and we are all incomparable beings."

Shortened versions for repeated journal writing, chanting at stop lights, notes posted on mirrors, and for relaxation/meditation — to be silently repeated on exhalation of each deep breath, for 10 breaths:

- "I am motivated by the excellence of others."
- "I am an incomparable being."
- "I am myself and growing."

2. *Initial negative thought:*
"I'm drying up. I can't give anymore. There's nothing left for me." (Notice the "all or nothing" belief system and the grandiose, overdramatic statements.)
Inner voice: "Hmmm . . . There it is

again. Stop!" (3 deep breaths) "Now, how can I use that material?"

Affirmations:

- "I am finding ways to give to others and still have enough for me."
- "I can give to others in efficient ways that help us all to grow."
- "I select wisely the ways to give."
- "I promote self-sufficiency in an atmosphere of love."

Notice that the affirmations are phrased . . .

1. In positive terms (not "I won't rescue . . ." but "I promote self-sufficiency . . .")
2. As if they are a present fact, not a future "wish" or "want," because the subconscious is more easily programmed thus to initiate action and to heal naturally.

The affirmative writings in this book are offered as supplement to your own process of transformation. The affirmations are written as "I" messages, nutritious food for the inner Wisdom. That Wisdom is always present and ready to hear its native tongue spoken. Each affirmation is followed by an inspirational passage to bolster your courage, to help you keep your face turned toward the light and to love the light within.

It is a privilege to share these cries of hope, cries that were born of pain and passed through labor of love and faith to become songs, sacred songs for strength on the hero's journey.

May the steps of your journey be eased and enlivened and may you well remember what a miracle you are.

*I have much to offer and much to enjoy —
I deserve to be well and happy.*

Believe that you have paid enough for your mistakes, and know the healing power of self-forgiveness. Lift the burden of your suffering and self-punishment from yourself and from the world. Love yourself, accept love, put yourself in the way of joy and you will automatically begin to rise toward becoming a more healthy and nourishing member of Earth's hopeful loving force.

*I am loveable. I love the way
I _____ .*

Are you "love-able" — able to receive love? When was the last time you gave yourself a pat on the back or let a compliment soak in?

Know that it is within your power to shape yourself to a significant degree. To whatever you attend will come energy and strength. Attend the best aspects of yourself and those qualities will grow more real and robust, more admirable and you more loveable.

JANUARY 3

*I am in daily touch with my assets
and fine qualities.*

Take inventory; you will be amazed and
enheartened by what you discover. Make
actual lists of your assets, adding items
whenever you feel successful, helpful, loving,
joyful, creative, healthy or otherwise positively
alive — even in small amounts. Listen carefully to compliments, read between the lines,
keep adding to your lists.

If you are depressed, recall a time when
you felt more alive and powerful and energetic, more like doing and trying — record
your assets at that time. Let all of this lift you
up to a reality-based perspective of who you
are and what you have to offer. Only then can
you approach full effectiveness at enhancing
our world.

JANUARY 4

I am deserving right now of the best the universe has to offer.

Look at a new baby — that fragile, fresh wellspring of love and power and purpose. Such promise! We want the best for that little Earth-mate. Would you want her to ever degrade herself in any way? Of course not! Each new being has the birthright of sprouting and maturing in the fertile ground of abundant love and self-confidence.

Remember that you were once such a shining child. That child still lives in you. You still deserve the best and have the capacity to give that inner child excellent nurturing. Allow yourself to create your life as a work of art, a work of love, just as you would want for a new child.

JANUARY 5

The real self within me is attractive and magnetic.

You need wear no masks nor pretend. Risk being still; be quiet, wait. See what emerges in a relationship or in a group without an effort at being "somebody." Or be louder, allow yourself to bubble over a little, if your habit is to be too often silent. Become a patient witness. Give yourself some time. After all, the roles and habits and tricks for gaining acceptance took a long time to gather. They will fall away slowly and there will be *You,* slightly more vulnerable, eventually much less afraid.

*I am valuable and loveable even though
not everyone loves me.*

Is there anyone you love who is not loved
by everyone else, who is not even liked by
some people? Of course, there is! Allow
yourself the same courtesy and avoid being
hard on yourself when there is evidence that
you are not highly esteemed by some. Do not
base your self-concept on the myth that one
must be loved and admired by everyone at all
times. (Few of us actually believe this in our
rational minds, yet feelings indicate some
level of incorporation of the myth.) Work
instead on closing the gaps that you create in
your own self-affection. Healthy self-love is
the basis of hearty other-love. Self-respect and
self-care furnish energy for loving someone.
And when you are loving, you are very
valuable.

I am a creation as splendid as a mountain,
the stars, the breaking waves.
I am a special kind of miracle.

You are every bit as wonderful as the most intricate snowflake, the most radiant sunset. You are a conscious expression of life, a miraculous arrangement of stardust with spirit and intellect and love. Never forget the glory of the gift of your essence. Whatever happens, the spark remains and it can ignite your beauty again and again.

I learn from each life step I take.
There really are no mistakes.

Relationships end; jobs or enterprises don't work out; important plans face dead ends. You may be tempted to call them mistakes, catalog them among your lists of failures. Instead look upon these events as opportunities to learn about living, about the way you mesh gears with the machinery of life. Try to take such situations a little less seriously. Trust that you will rise again and start looking for the lessons. Search out the patterns so you may better understand your values, your needs, your habits, your addictions, your strengths and weaknesses. Then you will know what to change and what to cherish.

Today, I am forgiven
for _____ .

Forgive yourself. Have faith that others will forgive you. Believe that you can relax in that faith, resting in the surety of your natural drive to become more loving, more effective, more of what you want. There is no need for self-punishment, only awareness and acknowledgment of steps in the right direction.

JANUARY 10

*I can embrace myself and discover my
uniqueness again and again.*

Your sacred duty is to love yourself well.
There are times when you may hold within
your powerful grasp a fragile Earth-child —
your own green self, sprouting under the
winter soil. Be your own good parent, nurture
your newness with warm soft rain and gentle
winds. Be compassionate with yourself. You
are a wakeful flowing expression of your
universe, especially created to learn and to
love. You are very special.

JANUARY 11

*I expand and my light becomes brilliant
as I accept nurturing and
validation from others.*

Allow yourself to be cared for; ask for help and tenderness; accept it. Accept the smiles, the greetings, the evidences that you are recognized. Choose the parts of compliments that you are able to fit into your self-image and consciously construct a fine and beautiful self-concept.

*I am competent at joyfully claiming
my best qualities.*

You are the very best person to monitor
you. Pick out what you like and tell yourself
about it. Tell a friend, too. Say something like,
"I'm so proud that I . . ." Include some ways
you just *are*, not only what you *do*. Enjoy
yourself! It will become easier as you practice
and thrive.

*I have done the best that I could. No matter
what has gone before, I am capable of
a multitude of improvements.*

To despise yourself at any time only saps
your energy. You need all your energy to pull
yourself up, to get on your right and chosen
way. Relax your jaw, melt those uptight
muscles, take a deep breath and let the self-
doubt go. Nurse your future, not your injured
pride. Pull yourself a little taller and know that
in the pain, the last facade has fallen and you
are ready for a better you.

JANUARY 14

*I can feel good about myself even if
someone disapproves.*

Believe in yourself. Do not allow your self-image and your convictions to sway wildly in the ill wind of negative criticism. And take care not to imagine criticism where there is merely mild questioning or honest delivery of information. Often you have done the very best you could. Be a careful judge of the value of the feedback you receive, culling out the chaff and planting only those golden seeds that will ripen into self-esteem and wisdom.

*In full awareness I graciously accept
the gifts from each of my
personal qualities.*

You might have labelled yourself as stubborn, for example. Labels can fossilize, so stir things up a bit and examine all the rising aspects. Stubborn might also connote firm, tenacious, full of conviction — fine attributes when hanging in there is the best policy. Accept these empowerments and then take care to temper it with flexibility when being stubborn is foolish. Accept the gifts in total consciousness. Be selective and build a more beautiful and loving you.

JANUARY 16

*I measure the growth of my self-esteem
in the loving quality of my listening.*

When you can hear silently the tale of
another's journey through territory familiar to
you, that is a triumph. It is such a temptation
to fill the air with, "I know . . ." or "I've
already been there, so here is *my* story . . ." or
"Here is my wisdom, take heed . . ." When
you rest secure in your own Selfhood, you
listen, taking pride in their new knowing,
their progress — empowering, not over-
powering; lighting the way, without casting
shadows. It is a true test and you are surely
worthy.

*I am still worthy and valuable
when I make a mistake.*

You are not ruined or worthless when you
make mistakes. To degrade yourself, in
addition to other consequences, is to pay a
price too high. Save your energy, preserve
your integrity for the necessary restorations.
Leave yourself intact and send yourself inspiring messages.

*I am capable of controlling
my habits.*

From deep within comes the finest help
you can receive for overcoming harmful
habits and dependencies. You are the only
one with the self-knowledge and the motivation to free yourself. You can find help,
support, relaxation and nutrition train-
ing . . . everything you need to engineer your
own good health. What finer way to use your
intelligence and creativity.

*I have the right to exist without
proving anything.*

When you are not so often seeking approval
or outside certification of your right to be
alive and well, there will be so much more of
you available for loving others. And, of course,
you *are* a being with a core of divinity, a
shining spirit — no matter how separated
from this you may feel. It is there, deep
within, ready to be reached; and that perfect
essence of you has every right to exist in joy
and to reach fulfillment. Take courage and
have faith in the central beauty that is yours as
you more completely liberate the best of you.
Do this for yourself and for the greater love
you will have to offer, not to prove your worth
to anyone. Your value is already proven, the
most precious birth-gift. It only remains to be
more fully realized.

*I am honest as I assess my situation.
I can face it, stop blaming others and make
a wise decision based on accurate
self-evaluation.*

You can look at your past behaviors and choices, find the patterns and decide to change the habits, especially if they have led you repeatedly into corners. You can be justly proud of yourself for not avoiding any shards of evidence, for stalking the traces of less sensible moves. You are fully capable of finding the strength of self-esteem to be truthful with yourself and still know your own value. Such is the stuff of a heroic life; and we are all heroes who remain hopeful, honest and full of good humor in hard times.

*I recognize the rise in my self-esteem when
I listen and celebrate the
success of others.*

You can learn to avoid tooting your own
horn when others are celebrating their accomplishments, insights and victories. Your
sense of self need not depend so much on
other-recognition that you cannot wait a while
to share yours. And it is certainly a satisfying
function to be holding the spotlight for a
friend.

I can step out of my ego and witness
myself lovingly and accurately.
I notice that I am a person who
<u>*(is . . . or does . . .)*</u> *.*

You have so much to gain from accurate
self-observation and personal inventory.
There is no conceit in honest acceptance of
your adequacy and excellence. There need be
no shame admitting even large imperfections.
You can be sure others have noticed. It is
magical thinking to believe that hiding
anything from yourself makes it invisible also
to others. That seems a little like a baby
playing peek-a-boo who assumes those little
hands that block her own view also hide
herself wholly. Be brave. Take ownership of
your power — admit to your assets and best
qualities and face the need for change.
Shaping up can be a grand adventure. You
have nothing to lose but your blinders.

*I accept with courage
the imperfections in myself.*

Approximation of perfection and the maintenance of that position is quite a burden. Relieve yourself of such a debilitating load. Observe without shame the discrepancies between what is and what could be. Accept the reality of limitations; accept some grief at disappointments and move quickly on. Do not be surprised at consistently going beyond those boundaries.

*I am in touch with my center —
my place of inner stillness,
wisdom, strength and courage.*

Stay in touch. Never stray far from your center of peace, power, utter belief in love, beauty and goodness. Practice a pattern of breathing, a position of fingers, a syllable, a prayer — whatever will take you there. Do what you must to always leave a path cleared, portals open for passage to this place of true peace, this refuge, this portable home of all homes.

JANUARY 25

*I am demonstrating responsibility for
my choices and claiming my
positive personal power.*

Give yourself hearty credit for your ability
to think, to say No, to assess accurately the
difference between what you know will
happen and what you imagine, to recognize
differences between inability (can't) and
emotional choice (won't), to make choices
rather than march like a robot to the programming of your should's. You are a powerful
human being in control of your own reality,
operating at your own pace, in your own
unique way. Allow no one to discount that
potency.

*I am empowered by bold images
of what I really want.*

Do not be fooled by what you have come to expect that you ought to want. Envision scenarios of various alternatives and note your feelings — a little thrill, fear, heart-pounding in excitement, resignation, dullness. Notice your patterns of recurring interest, involvement, investment. When you know (and from a reservoir of inner wisdom you will know), allow yourself time each day to create strong encouraging imagery. Make it as fully real as possible in your mind. Build wholly in your imagination the conditions you truly desire in your life. Enjoy the feelings. Know that you are self-programming for success. Doors will begin to open.

*I can be basically hopeful and optimistic
and still need to ventilate feelings
from time to time.*

Life has many hardships co-existing sturdily
among the delights. Most of us have suffered
heavy losses. Everyone will. To attempt a
constant cheerful demeanor is to live a lie.
Even the most mentally healthy person will
feel the need to express confusion, dismay,
sadness or anger; and will have periods of
burn-out, depression and malaise. To dwell
long with these feelings is dangerous. To
deny them and force them to hide somewhere among vital organs is possibly more
perilous. Find harmless ways to ventilate and
feel no guilt about it. Ask your friends to help.

JANUARY 28

*I am opening emotional space
for feeling good.*

You can become highly proficient at determining if the pain you bear is truly part of an
upward journey or if it serves no positive
purpose. Hear the message of your discomfort. Does it speak of rewards to come? Assess
their probable worth balanced against loss of
present joy. How likely is a pay-off? Be a
careful detective. Uncover some clues and
possibly abandon situations creating superflu-
ous suffering. Become expert at ridding
yourself of unnecessary pain.

In my loneliness, I recognize fertile
fields for sowing new seeds of
love and service.

Being alone can offer healing sanctuary. When loneliness does set in, however, it may be an indication of an opening in your life, a space for the creation of entirely new relationships and ways of being available to others. Perhaps it is time to reach out in places you never thought of before. Be creative and ride through the pain of loneliness to a rebirth of enthusiasm.

*I can grieve from time to time and still be
a happy person. My grief is a cleansing.
My tears are the holiest of water,
blessing the depth of my caring.
My cries are a song of reality.*

It is possible to grieve a little each day — to
feel a brotherly tug at heart for the squirrel
who knew too little of streets; to long for lost
friends; to wish again for what might have
been; to cry sorrowfully in pain for anything
loved and lost and beyond recall. Why not?
Why not release the grief? Why store it up to
tear away the softness inside? Let it loose
before the claws become too sharp, before
the growls echo too loudly and change your
very mind's vibrations. Yes, make your life's
work the continued creation of exuberance
and prosperity and love. But if there is
sadness, let it out, let it clear away and make
space for gladness.

JANUARY 31

*I can remain healthy in a challenging
situation, open to achieving
a broader perspective.*

It is often essential to simultaneously see a
situation from more than one viewpoint. Only
from such a broad-based vantage point can
you resolve conflicts and solve problems with
unbiased clarity. It takes time to gain such
unclouded insight, with defense mechanisms
on hold and a mind wide open to possibilities
— a sign of true intelligence.

*I have the right to be angry and
physically to rid myself of the excess
energy in appropriate ways.*

Free yourself from anger-tension, escape
the attacks on vital organs, leave the dilemma
of shout or pout. Destroy no one with your
anger, least of all yourself. There are alternatives for discharging the very real physical
anger response. Begin to discover a few.

You could run, jog, walk around the block
as fast as you can. Dance it out, clap or stomp
it out. Write it out or talk it out with a friend.
Execute a series of isometric exercises. Cool
off and then plan a constructive, caring
confrontation if it might help. (It might help.)
Follow your anger response to a positive pay-
off. Let it teach you something about yourself
and your reactions, your needs, your values.
Take the gift that is offered and it may not
return so often — anger.

*I am remembering the most basic values
of life; I am glad for whatever part
of those I have.*

Perhaps you fear that you have lost, or will
lose, much that is valuable to you. Often the
losses, though seeming truly awful, are not as
deep as you might think. When attempting to
place those losses in perspective in order to
make careful decisions, take stock of what
remains of these basics: your sanity, your
health, your wonder and curiosity, your ability
to laugh, your drive to offer something good
to others, your ability to love and to receive
love. (Remember, there are all kinds of love,
and many people needing love and wanting
to give it.) Focus on what you have of each
and begin to pick up the pieces, setting goals
for development in such basic areas of life.
Suddenly, your way may become more clear
and the future more shining.

I trust that there is always a way out.
I will discover it.

Your faith will oil the machinery. Your positive attitude and courage will cut easier paths. Program your powerful mind (conscious and subconscious) to deliver you into joy and then take some action. Every carefully made choice has a pay-off. Accept, learn and move ahead. Never give up.

My beauty survives. I give attention and energy to the good, no matter what.

Believe in the grace, the bloom, the enduring inner fire, the soft touch of one loved. Allow the consciousness of this to survive loss and the long cold season. Be lifted a little above sorrow and be of wholesome vision. Try seeing problems as challenges and return your focus to the search for love and wonder.

FEBRUARY 5

*I am capable of patience,
of flowing on through to a solution that
will be of long-term value.*

You have more stamina than you know.
Trust your hardy soul; accredit your own
ingenuity. You are courageous and can bear
some discomfort. You are capable of stem-
ming the urge for a quick fix. Relax a little,
bending like a strong sapling in the storm.
Give yourself time to find a way for more
lasting success.

FEBRUARY 6

*I will become quiet and calm, ready for
an answer to come from within.
I trust that I will know.*

Release the need to agonize over a decision. After a period of assessing strengths and
values, of gathering information, of rationally
decisioning, let it go. (And be sure to recognize choices; often a "can't" more accurately
translates to "won't.") Do not allow the
thinking about a decision to become obses-
sive. Relax, be still, allow it all to incubate for
a while in the warmth and richness of the total
You. When the airway is no longer cluttered
with compulsive thoughts, the pure, strong
voice of inner knowing can be heard.

I will feel only joy when someone else shines in an area of my own aspiration.

There is utterly no worth in permitting envy to rob you of peace. Remain centered and serene and know that you, too, will have your time to excel. Your carefully nurtured gifts will be offered and recognized and are not reduced as others offer theirs. Rejoice in the addition of new strength to something you value. Simply be glad and feel energized in co-operation.

FEBRUARY 8

*I am surely moving away from my
addictions, stepping high in new freedom.*

Some nonchemical addictions are potentially as damaging as the substances we call drugs. Notice the times when you feel terrible, awful, horrible or can't stand something. What is it that you can't stand having or not having in your life? Perhaps you are looking at an addiction. Root it out and examine it. Try reducing your severe need to the status of most favored option and watch your withdrawal pain turn to mere discomfort when things are not going as desired. Begin to really appreciate your liberation from negative reactions.

FEBRUARY 9

I am health-directed. I choose to be decisional, to relax, to move slowly.

If programmed consistently, your body/mind can learn to resist compulsions. Believe that you are full of strength and resolve and have faith in yourself. You will begin to take control and to be decisional about reaching for a healthier, more excellent life. You certainly deserve to step free. You can do it!

I remain well and complete
in the midst of change.

Change is a major rule of nature. Trust that the natural course of events will create change, that there will be handles presented for pulling out (and you will notice and take advantage of them) and that your own problem-solving process will move things along. Relax into the stretch and stay centered. Be grateful for what you do have. Gratitude is such a grand energizer.

*I confront my fears, allow them to help
me construct precautions and
go on to live fully.*

Speak openly with your fears. Ask them to
tell you all they know. You will be listening to
your own inner wisdom. Allow Fear and
Courage to engage in dialogue about a given
situation. Change refutations to questions and
draw out more detail. Merge the knowing and
live a wise adventure.

FEBRUARY 12

*I have a wellspring of peace, wisdom,
love and energy within.*

You have so much more than you know.
Brief thrills of joy, a rising of enthusiasm,
prickles of hope — all of these are hints at the
depths of possibilities below the surface of
your rich and full self. It is all there; you are
never truly empty. Even a profound stillness, a
quiet mood can be an unconscious waiting —
waiting for an upwelling. It will surely come if
you provide the space and take the pressure
off the well cap.

I do care; and I know that there is a way to feel good and productive, even jubilant, as I grow in personal potency.

You *can* pull out of apathy, walk away from despair and learn to feel vitally alive. Every breath you inspire from this moment on can help you become recharged, energized and full of hope. Your body/mind naturally yearns for life and for solutions to problems. Watch yourself begin to move ahead. Take heart and enjoy the journey.

*I am becoming more and more capable
of loving, beginning with myself
and reaching out.*

The ability to love others arises out of a deep, clear well of self-respect. Your precious body/mind, a masterfully created instrument of peace and good will, must be finely tuned and well cared for. Love yourself with daily fresh air, exercise and deep breathing, whole nourishing foods, adequate rest, laughter and investments of time in friendship. Take yourself to places of beauty, even if only a neighborhood park; spend time hallowing there. Recognize your own assets and strengths often. Notice your shortcomings without self-degradation, trusting that you will grow and make progress. When fellow pilgrims falter, you will listen without judgment, wisdom in restraint, drawing forth their beauty with your trust and your courage.

*I am lifted and illumined as I
skillfully nurture and validate others.*

Some of life's greatest joys can involve
creation of special bouquets. There are so
many ways to inspire another — a full sweet
hug, an unexpected greeting card, a single
bud, one dried leaf, help with some house-
work, yardwork, homework, child care,
granny care, any care. Be attuned. There is
plenty of brain capacity for storing the cues to
let you know just when and what would mean
the most.

Stay tuned to merit and mind the need for a
heartening word along the way to a goal.
Validate, substantiate and certify the behaviors
and qualities that will fertilize healthy self-
esteem. We all need that from one another.
We all are enriched as we share the courage.

FEBRUARY 16

*I am working in joyful partnership
with others.*

The growth or accomplishment of another
does not diminish you in any way. All of us
must be in collaboration as we progress. You
will find more and more ways to offer your
gifts and will find it increasingly appropriate
to encourage the development of others' gifts.
Allow your interactions and relationships to
be synergistic, everyone rising together to a
new level of energy and creation beyond the
sum of the parts.

*I can get what I want now
and support abundance for others.*

There are many ways to lovingly assert
yourself. One method involves simply stating
the effects on you of a particular situation,
being very specific and including possible
consequences (not threats), remembering
that downgrading another is counter-produc-
tive. Even when there is initial resistance,
creative bargaining and a refusal to be negative will reap surprising rewards.

*Love links us all. I am connected to many
and to much because I love.*

Love is the force that unites us all with the
harmony of the universe. Love lets you look
with the heart of a poet — seeing not things,
but the spirit, the essence of people and
things. Love lets you shed a tear at the fragile,
the hopeful, the unbearably beautiful, even if
you are a big, burly man or a smaller man
trying to be big or a woman trying not to be
over-sentimental. Love lets you touch someone with understanding, reaching out beyond
the doubts. Love allows you to let yourself be
touched. When you develop the capacity for
reverence and commit yourself to kindness,
you join with all that is good. You are part of
the gift and the giving.

*I am becoming more empathetic
and more direct.*

Becoming a truly whole person involves
developing a greater capacity for understanding others (and showing them) and for
knowing where you draw the line (and saying
so). You will grow rich and golden with
wisdom when you try to walk more often in
another's shoes. Instead of being toxic with
judgments, you will spread love. And in that
loving wisdom, you will be straight and
assertive when necessary to preserve your
integrity, your space, your Self. Empathy with
others, taking care of you — both lines of the
same full circle of skillful living.

*I solve problems. I seldom
punish myself or others.*

There can be infinitely more love in your
life when you know the difference between
punishment and problem-solving. Before
proceeding in a difficult situation, honestly
answer this question, "Do I want one or both
of us to hurt, or do I want us to discover a fair
and creative way to meet our various needs?"
This powerful choice is largely yours.

FEBRUARY 21

*I am grateful and capable of letting
others know of my gratitude.*

Personal growth involves acknowledging
your interdependence. Everyone who is still
functional in this world is receiving help and
nurturance from others. Honor the ones who
nurture you, even the mailman who still
smiles on sore feet, and especially the loved
one who remains and listens and shares. Be a
creative detective. Make a delightful un-game
of sleuthing for thank-you cases and caring
clues.

*I will look beyond the ideal fantasy
to find the true and hidden beauty
in a special relationship.*

Acceptance of what is begins the progress.
The next step is to understand how and why,
without blaming anyone. Finally, you may be
able to move forward together, taking constructive action for change. Building a beautiful relationship is a high act of co-creation.

I will allow only interest and positive
motivation when I note the differences
between myself and any other.
I am unique and we are all really
incomparable beings.

Comparisons of self to others serve no
useful purpose, especially if the result is a
superior or inferior attitude. Learn from the
grace and skill of others; allow such learning
to be uplifting. Let their shortcomings also be
your teacher; and remain bravely gentle.

FEBRUARY 24

*I can give to others and still
have enough for me.*

You are capable of excellent planning for
the most efficient use of resources, for
yourself and to help others. It is not necessary
to sacrifice your own joy and well-being and
chances for progress, nor is it desirable to
model self-sacrifice to others. Self-sacrifice
means loss of self to some degree. A major
goal must be to spread the ways of gaining full
life, not losing big chunks of it. You can be
generous and advance personally. Allow
yourself freedom from the "rescuer" role,
while inviting others to win pride as they
become more autonomous and strong.

*I will allow competition to do
only good things for me.*

Try a transformation. Change the basic
mind-set of competition to cooperation by
using any point of comparison as an exciting
stimulus to do your best. Winning (while
others lose) is a shallow basis for self-esteem.
Fearing a number two position or lower
consumes valuable energy. Dealing with a
perceived loss also wastes time and resources.
Let the excellence of others give you only
courage.

I love my fellow human beings.
I look within myself when I begin
to judge others harshly.

You must "be-(a)ware" of yourself as you begin to find fault in other people. You may be projecting your own impure motives and imperfections on others. What evidence do you truly have that the negative expectations are fair and well-founded? Consider the strength of positive expectations (people often live up or down to expectations) and of strong reinforcement of healthy behavior. Never underestimate the power of a gentle hug and several kind words. They are part of life's most brilliant silver lining.

I let go of my need to feel angry or
aggravated in most situations. I find joy in
helping other persons feel at ease
at difficult times.

You will continue to deal occasionally with those whose behavior seems irritating or maddening. In most cases, it will be a step on your journey to peace and wellness as you focus on what the other(s) may need in order to feel more comfortable and loved and open to possibilities. Often your defenses will seem less necessary as you seek to truly understand another. You may even find that what you were telling yourself is less than accurate. A new perspective can yield surprising payoffs.

*My personal center of peace, strength and
integrity remains stable within me,
even as I interact dynamically with others.*

In situations of loving connection or conflict, do not allow your center to be drawn
somewhere in the middle of you and the
other person(s); it is too easy to be pulled off
balance that way. Use the wisdom and understanding and potency that your center generates from deep within, remaining less vulnerable and more capable of calling forth the
best in everyone.

*I am letting people know how much
I love them.*

The expression of love and support for one
another, without immediate or expected
return, sets us higher and higher above self-
absorption. We honestly approach the angelic
when there is no holding back out of false
pride or laziness. Demonstrate to someone
right away that you notice, you appreciate, you
care. To do so is to offer a pure hymn of
celebration of the good.

*I can forgive   (a special person)   for
not being ideal. I am tolerant
and full of love.*

You know the truth — no one really
parallels the ideals we set for significant
others. Avoid punishments, in word and deed,
when you discover disturbing shortcomings.
No one exists to please you. Each human
being is fashioning a life — an incredibly
challenging task. Your choices may be only
how best to communicate your preferences,
to validate what you perceive as improvements and finally to go about building your
own vital and significant life.

I can listen . . . patiently, silently,
blamelessly, shamelessly.
I can listen with love.

You are extremely capable of hearing the story of another without judging or defending. Stifle the need to feel one-up or the urge to be one-down. Listen. Hear it all. See and feel the other person's essence flowing out and pouring all around in priceless sounds. Whatever the content, the floodgates are at least partly open, communication has begun. Know that the gates may slam shut again. Keep them open. Breathe deeply and stay afloat, neither condemning nor defending; listening, hearing more than words; learning who really talks and gestures and sighs and speaks so far beyond syllables. When you have truly heard and checked what you have heard against the reality of the other, wait for more. Then tell your side or offer an opinion. Perhaps by then, you need say very little at all.

MARCH 4

When I serve with love,
I am magnificent.

When you choose to make life easier for someone, to spread love and comfort and enrichment as a service, you are never subjugated or abased. Whatever work you do, if done with love, it is noble and free.

I preserve love as I enhance the
dignity of all human beings.

Wherever the integrity and esteem of another person is increased, there is love. Shaming and belittling are a reduction of the love force, no matter what the perceived goal. You are full of wisdom about ennobling and enabling others.

*I am a miraculous expression of life,
and life is the most splendid
blossom of the universe.*

Indeed, you are a miracle! Feel the sparkling air on clean skin of a winter morning. Notice the way your functioning organs work. Appreciate the smooth operations of your kidneys, your lungs, your eyes, your ears. Be still and be thankful for the beating of your heart. Learn where all your vital organs are located and become their friend. They have certainly been yours. If any of these precious parts are not fully functioning right now, close your eyes, take your attention inside and imagine those organs surrounded, cradled, loved in healing golden-white light. Feel yourself becoming more tuned to a plentitude of new alternatives for nurturing the miracle that is you. In your growing awareness, more fully honor your sacred responsibility to make the most of this gift — your life.

*I forgive myself for not being
all that I expected.*

Self-healing requires forgiveness, and none
can be truly forgiven before yourself. Face
squarely your perceived shortcomings, unex-
aggerated, and use them to fashion goals for a
brighter future, full of love and laughter and
constructive action. No good can come of self-
torture, of chronic guilt, of constant regret.
Those ogres only nourish the aches and pains,
the ulcers and the cancers and the heart
attacks. Take full, deep breaths. With each
exhalation let a disappointment go, and
breathe in deeply the fresh freedom of self-
forgiveness. Move forward energetically into
grace.

*I forgive others for not
being as I expected.*

People can often grow to meet realistic positive expectations, generously fed with appreciation. However, expectations can be inappropriate, generating pain and conflict. Never enslave yourself to the tyranny of enforcing your own demanding presumptions. Allow the role of expectations in your life to be only nourishing, not diminishing, as you build yourself and those you touch with trust and confidence. Spread about more support than criticism. Love the others as they make their journey, and know that you heal yourself with that love. Let your byword become encouragement and be radiant with hope, be rising in self-reliance.

MARCH 9

*I forgive life for not being
as I expected.*

Let the crumbled bits of your dreams
become rich compost for a new garden, full of
well-founded hopes and fresh plans. Be glad
you have dreamed; your yearning has always
yielded more, if only an awareness of something beyond. Use your energy now, not
turned inward with searing regret nor outward
in seeking revenge, but forward — reaching
for the best that can be yours. Waste not a
moment more. Dance forward, be brave. Face
life as it is and is not, and make it more.

MARCH 10

I accept with courage the
imperfections in my world.

At any given time there may be rain on the picnic, ducks out of line, problems to be tackled. These events and conditions must not be constantly experienced as disappointments, but as integral parts of life — challenges to build muscles on, to learn from, to grow with in grace and wisdom. Stop fighting what is, cease blaming and use your vital forces to set up a far better tomorrow.

MARCH 11

I forgive _____
for _____ .

Who is it that you need to forgive now, so that you may remove the burrs from your insides? Maybe it is yourself. Maybe it is a special person who did not live up to your expectations long ago. The choice may be quite obvious; or perhaps there are partly hidden resentments. Root them out, acknowledge them and let them go. Be in peace and wellness as you practice forgiveness.

MARCH 12

*What is right for me will pay off
for others in the long run.*

A life of sacrifice can be a costly forfeit. The
losses may be heavy — loss of the twinkle in
your eye, loss of zeal, loss of an original life,
loss to the world of a primary creator. Know
that your self-discovery and self-fulfillment are
also other-constructive, world-constructive.
Used-up persons often cannot still the resent-
ful urges; turned outward they weaken and
destroy; turned inward they create illness —
so no one benefits. Go now, reach out for that
which yields for you a healthy glow. Your light
will illuminate the strength of others and
everyone you shine upon will feel renewed.

I can be in control of stress.
I can either eliminate the stressors in
my life or cope appropriately
with those that remain.

Begin to monitor yourself. Do you deny or avoid dealing with the stressors in your life? If so, you may notice yourself suffering from chronic respiratory problems. Do you over-intellectualize and "rationalize-away" your distress? You may find yourself with an ulcer or another digestive disorder. Do you worry; over-do and constantly mentally rehearse in order to stay on top of things? Your symptom may be high blood pressure. You are ready now to reach out for the skills that are best for you — perhaps assertiveness, time-management, goal-setting, learning to check the reality of the stories you tell yourself, relaxation and deep-breathing techniques. Stay aware of yourself and your habits.

I am fully alive NOW.
*I am finding fresh ways to be
vital and new.*

There is so much to learn and experience
and no time to lose. Try one new thing today
— magnitude is of no importance. Novelty
rejuvenates, creates new connections within a
fertile mind. Know that there are no guarantees and that there always exists the possible
let down. Disappointment is never lethal;
relax and resist less. It will pass mildly and
you will have known its name beforehand. No
surprises, but joy when things are fine.

*There is a flip side to everything.
I remain whole and unfragmented even
amidst a universe of opposites, even
among my own disparate qualities.*

This is not an either/or universe. There is a
bright side and a dark side of the moon. There
is creation and destruction, implosion and
explosion. There is life and there is death,
pain and ecstasy, laziness and drive, love and
hate, joy and despair, cowardice and heroism
— all within your world, within the world of
you. To deny or ignore any of it is to become
shattered. Allow a union of the nations within
you, let the polarities co-exist peacefully,
create of them a whole-some world of Self —
spherical and full and changing, dynamic and
totally alive!

*I rejoice in the happiness and
blessings of others.*

If a high part of your purpose is to enhance
the lives of others, as well as your own, then
that function is actualized as you celebrate
and increase the occasions of others' joy and
success. Envious and jealous reactions only
diminish you, in your heart and in the eyes of
the world. Self-esteem and mutual admiration
flourish in a garden of generous recognition
of your fellows' good fortune, talent and
achievement.

I am inspired by each breath I take.

Have you ever thought about the connection? To "inspire" is to breathe in; to "be inspired" is to feel renewed, full of life and hope. Our breath is our constant link with life. Keep breathing; deeply, slowly, rhythmically. Stay full of newness; stay kindled and alive.

MARCH 18

*I accept the messages that my body
sends and I am sending my body beautiful
messages. I see myself becoming more
 (Describe a positive change as if it is
 happening.)*   .

Listen to your body; do not be guilty of
"ignore-ance." Be in tune, sensitive, aware. Be
willing to alter some behaviors and attitudes
in order to create a more marvelous total self.
And know the potency of your words and
messages to you. Be selective of the images
projected on your mental screen. Give yourself the priceless gift of beautiful, caring
words of encouragement; hopeful, radiant
images. You can become just what you tell
yourself to become. You will begin to place
energy in carrying out the programming you
provide yourself. You will make consistently
fine choices.

I am being gentle with myself.

You have every right to invest time in changing any system that requires you to be violent to yourself, including your own habits of overwork or overindulgence. It does not build good character to damage your body/self: to consistently ignore the needs to empty your bladder, not to stretch overcontracted and cramped muscles, nor to quench your thirst for healthy fluids, to loosen your belt and expand with deep breaths of life-giving air. The only sensible way to be is gentle with the best friend you can ever have — yourself. Let that valuable person rest and eat nutritious foods. Allow that blessed creation to laugh and move and to have times of quiet relaxation. Stop kicking yourself for making mistakes, for imperfections. Set positively stated goals with small steps, guaranteeing many successes.

I embrace life, hold it close, and love it.

There is always something to celebrate. Even in loneliness and boredom, there are still babies at the grocery store and leaves like stained glass when the sun shines through them. Even when life seems a fierce imbecile, you can tame it and raise it with a gentle touch, a simple gift, a letter full of fun. Look for life's smiles around every corner, behind each cloud. If there seems to be none, give it a little tickle.

MARCH 21

I am able to recognize the love that is being offered to me.

Often the forms in which love comes to you may not match your fantasies. The offerings may not fit the mold. Be careful not to miss any of it; presume love to be there in all gestures, unless emphatically proven otherwise. Such an attitude will invite more love than you ever imagined.

MARCH 22

*I am a valuable human being, fully worthy
of a quality existence.*

It is not necessary for you to keep proving
yourself worthy to exist. So relax; be calm.
Cease the "How am I doing?" song and dance,
the "Please think I'm OK!" jitterbug. Relieve
yourself of those jitters and be at peace with
your own being. Everyone has the right to be.
Remain quiet and observe more, listen more.
The world is such a fascinating place when
you forget to "prove" yourself. Remember all
the others who so badly need recognition,
and you will already be filling a high purpose.

MARCH 23

I can openly face my anxieties and my least loveable qualities and still feel worthy of a beautiful existence.

It is unnecessary to hide from yourself in order to feel deserving. Apprehension about measuring up and negative self-diagnosis need not shake you from your center of calm assurance and belief in your abilities. Transform it all into shining goals and cheer yourself on with each brave stride.

I am capable now of living fully.

Be still. Take this moment. It is yours. Feel the air in circulating currents on your skin. Now go — find another miracle and rejoice. Make them longer, fuller — those miracles. Be full of the goodness of living. You can begin now the feast of being alive and begin anew every hour.

I am well.

Your body/mind/spirit — your total self-being responds at a deep level to your image of you as well or not well. Be well. Focus on what is working; celebrate, expand, rejoice in all that is well. Look there and the rest will follow. Send yourself encouraging messages — courage is what it takes to build a healthy self.

MARCH 26

I am giving myself excellent care so I may remain healthy and happy.

Your priceless body/mind is your greatest treasure. Protect it, polish and enhance it, investigate its immense value. Every hour spent in learning and doing healthful acts will likely be redeemed in years of greater vitality and effectiveness. Become proud of the assertive way you are guiding your own destiny — take control of your own well-being.

I am making my body a beautiful temple.

You may enter the circle of self — body/
mind/spirit — at any point and create whole,
healthy change. Achieve greater control and
more flexible use of your precious body and
automatically open doors to the intellect and
to the soul, take the reins of your emotions
and become fully alive.

MARCH 28

I may continuously return to my Divine Center, a sanctuary of inner calm.

In any situation, you have the capability of turning inward for peace and strength and wisdom. Simply withdraw from thought or action for a few seconds and focus on the part of yourself that feels like a stable, tranquil center. Draw your breath there and feel that place energized. Invest a few heartbeats of time in this place and win the serenity and wisdom for loving, appropriate action.

MARCH 29

I am calm.

You are a deep well of peace. You will become more and more efficient at reaching the center of stillness within. You are already calming when you become aware of muscles that are tight and surrender the tension, letting go of that negative sort of control. You are tranquil with every full breath you exhale; with each unsettling thought that floats away unfinished, you are calm.

I am healed.

You are taking the best possible care of yourself. With each deep breath, each longer stride, every bite of fresh fruit and vegetables, your body is revitalized. All laughs and affirmations, all moments of appreciation are healing your whole self. You are healed every moment that you believe you are.

MARCH 31

I am doing the best I can, right now.

Stop giving yourself such a hard time. Relax and trust your higher self to continue to emerge, to draw you upward, to create a finer life, to love more perfectly every day. Focus on what you are doing well, on what is working. Be glad.

*I accept the message this dis-ease
offers me as a gift.*

Speak with your pain, your discomfort, your
illness. Ask what it may be telling you. How
should you alter your lifestyle, your attitudes,
your relationships in order to be more
healthy? Create a realistic internal dialogue.
Contact the inner wisdom. Listen.

APRIL 2

I have the right to be unpredictable.

Be a surprise! Try something you never thought you would do, be, think or feel, especially if much of what you have been doing is habit, and most especially if something is clearly not working. Shake up old patterns and be different, be novel, be new and be stimulated into better health.

I have the right to laugh and have fun.

Belly laughs are the best of medicine. Everyday should promise laughter and hold the possibility of play, play that does not depend on winning for satisfaction, play that nourishes the happy child inside you. It is that child that sparks your imagination, that keeps your wonder alive, that is a joyful lover. Set a goal to nourish yourself more often with fun.

APRIL 4

*I have the right to ask for
what I want and need.*

Expect no one to read your mind. Expect
instead to reveal and to negotiate. Enjoy the
process, remaining an observant witness, of
your own drama, nonjudging, learning, giving,
receiving.

APRIL 5

*I have a dream. That dream gives
strength to my soul and is a beacon
that lights my way.*

Your world-dream is the nurturance of your
spirit. It has long been with you — the
magnificent way you see yourself offering
your gifts to the world. It matters not whether
you ever fully achieve it — only that it leads
you forward, a Johnny Appleseed of hope and
love and progress. Take note of all the seeds
you have dropped along the way. Define and
redefine your dream, again and again. Over
and over list even the smallest ways you have
made it real. Your dream has been guiding
you for a very long time, and it will lead you
on in a special kind of glory.

APRIL 6

I let go of the past.

Be creative; for you are a major creator of your life, your self. Strive to make that creation a masterpiece. Engineer the changes that are necessary for your health and happiness. Build the bridges, move forward in grace and peace. Your energy will sparkle and surge if you can then let go — release all the hatred and the blame, produce the space for love.

APRIL 7

*I am comfortable with things that
I do not fully understand.
I become more intelligent as I open
myself to new possibilities.*

The world is full of mystery. Scientists continue to dislodge old "proofs" and to discover more and more, the essence of which none may ever truly fathom. Your own experience should be teaching you that there are very few, if any, facts. There are far more secrets, beautiful and awe-full puzzles — full of challenge for the brave who refuse to close their minds around some small segment of truth. Be daring and full of excitement — keep exploring, never stop searching.

*I accept the extremes of a situation,
or within myself, as necessary segments
of the encircling truth.*

Do not succumb to confusion and conflict
when confronted with evidence of polarities.
A whole life will always include tendencies
toward staying and straying, seeking and
settling, loving and hating, cowering and
conquering, laughing and crying, trusting and
binding — often at the same time. There is no
craziness involved, merely normal knowing of
the poles of two hemispheres. Bring yourself
more solidly toward the equator, staying
mostly in the temperate zones, with fewer
jaunts to the far north and south. In other
words, accept the wide variations, don't fight
them. Use them to gain more perfect balance.

APRIL 9

In my drive toward self-transformation,
I will include others in the love,
the joy, the wonder I find
in being alive.

Taking the reins of a life of individual development will not send you galloping away from others. The richness you bring will provide many points of connection and your best will draw out their excellence. Your excitement will energize them. Happiness cannot isolate itself.

APRIL 10

*I welcome the innocence of
my fresh ideas.*

When you take time to hope, to dream, to emerge from the shell of your aloof coolness into the vigor of unfettered thinking, there will be crazy ideas. There will be wonderful, jazzy, strange, itty-bitty, sleek and pretty, headstrong, hopeless but inspiring, wild ideas. This is the stuff of progress. Do not be shy. Let them out to circulate, perhaps to couple happily with someone else's happy brainchildren.

*I am actualizing the potential and
possibilities within me.*

If you have poems on little slips of paper in
a shoe box — pull them out, type one and slip
it into a birthday card for someone you love.
He or she will be enriched. Do not hide your
talents because you might be embarrassed or
because someone else might feel envious.
The only reason humankind has flourished is
the courage of those who have risked expos-
ing their gifts. Not everyone writes poetry, of
course, but few of us share all that we might.
What are you hiding in your dream closet?
What interests have you always yearned to
follow? What abilities are waiting to be
sharpened? This life may be your only chance.
Do not wait too long to try. And you cannot
fail; for the adventure of the finding and the
giving is the pulse of life, not the accolades.

*I am reaching toward new goals, even as
I value what is real for me now.*

Know what you want. Dream it, say it,
stretch for it, like a vine climbing to the sun.
In the meantime, love your aliveness, give
talent and joy to what you are doing *now.* Do
not wallow in wanting; rather trust your
wisdom and your yeasting urges to move you
toward your dreams in peace.

APRIL 13

*I am thoughtful and careful
in decision-making.*

Do you know what set of values is the basis
for most of your decisions? Have you assessed
your own risk-taking behavior? Are you
security-based or adventure-bound? Do you
avoid risk at all costs or go for it often? Do you
gather information and examine the validity
of your sources? Do you simply wait for
something to happen, making it unnecessary
to decide? If so, do you consciously choose to
abdicate this way? It is certainly worth your
time to learn to make decisions.

I see myself becoming a fully functioning, fully actualized, highly evolved human being.

You can envision yourself using your talents, following your vital interests, being in full love and joy in your world. Form a picture on your mental screen of the self you want to be: doing, feeling, speaking, perceiving, moving, creating. Image yourself being this way for 10 minutes each day. Be perfectly comfortable and relaxed, breathe deeply and enjoy the show. Especially enjoy the results.

APRIL 15

I am wholly in love with this moment.

Allow a marvelous moment to stand alone
— apart from expectations, aside from negative self-image or habits of thought created by
past disappointments. Just let it be for now.
And be strengthened by it. Let such moments
be added to your image of the world and your
world will begin to conform to that inspiring
image. Be lifted when it is time to be lifted
and let nothing stand in your way. Float in the
blessed arms of freedom — freedom to be
fully alive in a blissful present.

APRIL 16

My life is full of exciting possibilities.
I am developing the competence
to make them happen.

Your greatest challenge is to be aware of the corridors and portals to higher fulfillment. Stay alert and confident. There will be surprising opportunities. You will know where to go to gain the skills to make things happen. Never be afraid to ask, to learn, to change.

*I can build for myself more encouraging
perceptions of my reality.*

A great deal of your reality depends upon
what you tell yourself about an experience or
an anticipated event. Much anger, for example, is unnecessary if you tell yourself that a
particular person, instead of being insensitive
and abrasive, is simply a pilgrim on a challenging life journey. Then it is easy to imagine
how to help correct the situation instead of
how to hurt a fellow traveler.

*I feel the stirrings and the promise
of springtime.*

There is promise in the rich soil over-
turned. Waiting seeds know what comes. Be a
part of the sweet urgency of spring. Notice the
excitement of birds; their singing lifts the chill
and moves your heart to wing. Forms do
change and the new blossoms always come.

I am aware.
I often choose positive thoughts
and communication.

You are not controlled by a runaway mind (or mouth). Relax and breathe deeply; wait; *decide* to either spend time and energy on a thought or to let it go. Find yourself with a clear mind, more serenity and much greater effectiveness.

*I am a visionary. I can see beyond
what now seems to be real.*

Appearances are not the reality; and reality includes recognition of what can be. Problems may be openings to new worlds. Those fantasies of excellence anywhere in your experience might be brought to fuller realization. Sweep the horizon, search from the stones to the stars, widening the breadth of your vision. Dream, scheme, build a sweeter world.

APRIL 21

I may be waiting; and I will allow
myself to be happy while I wait.

The future is not nailed down, even for those who seem to have it made. Reality often alters the firmest of plans. So fill your waiting with experience, with friends, with joy. Fill it with exploring and dancing and learning who you are. You will then be fully quickened when the time arrives for the waiting to end and the moves to begin.

*Just as the earth heals herself again and
again, I am healing myself now.*

Soon the recent road cut will wear a coat of
soft new green. Abandoned piles of sand and
soil will be graced with sunflowers; birds will
carry more seeds there and so will the wind.
Fox grows fat and strong after a starving snow.
So, too, you are healing all wounds, growing
in vitality, enlivened by a blooming hope.
Focus on the "springing" earth and when the
joy of this echoes even faintly in your heart,
give it attention and energy. Feel it grow.

*I have gifts to give. I will give
them and be fulfilled.*

Relax and be assured that your gifts will
emerge, demanding to be given, flowing forth
naturally, without extensive pressure on
yourself. These special offerings may not take
the form you once thought. Be careful not to
ignore something you have to give because it
does not fit some preconceived notion.
Observe yourself; witness your urges to give;
watch what you do offer; search for patterns
and learn to enhance and enrich your giving
— perhaps evolving into a life mission. Be
lifted by it all and be glad.

*Everything I learn is the basis for
new connections. I am open and ready for
the dawn of new knowledge.*

You can never learn enough, and yet
everything you learn is enough. Each observation brings you closer to life; every old person
heard, all encyclopedias opened are portals to
fuller being. Pick up a feather and wonder
about it; ask and read; look and listen and fly.

There is a place for me. I am finding it;
that is part of my life work.

You may sometimes feel displaced, an expatriate of sorts, the proverbial square peg. Spend a few moments in the warm sun, see the shadows dance on tree trunks, stand beneath a crescent moon, chuckle at a small child's laughter — and know it is well that you be here now. You belong to the worship-full moment. Make more such moments and so fertilize your spirit.

*I can create my own reasons and meaning
for life. Those reasons will most
probably be excellent and true.*

A fully alive individual will always search for more meaning, for more robust reasons. There is no shame in reaching beyond the found criteria for a right existence. Use your blooming awareness, your upward spiraling mind and be a builder. Make of inherited beliefs constructive material and then erect a grand cathedral of your creative loving theories.

*I have a goal. I reaffirm it often and
it gives me wings. My goal is*

———————— .

It is necessary for the human spirit to move
forward, to spiral upward, to soar somewhere
— to progress toward a goal. Redefine your
goals often, making sure they still fit you.
Remind yourself of their presence. Dedicate
yourself again and again. Then observe the
magic, the lift, the energy that can only
happen when your subconscious (your secret
pal if you program it right) subtly guides you
toward what you know you really want.

APRIL 28

I accept the best that life has to offer.

Reach out for the jewels — a deep lungful of crisp spring air, a hearty bear hug, a good cry, the mystery of a midnight thunderstorm, open and honest communication . . . There is so much to savor. Be born to it new each morning. It is all your gift.

I am a patient witness of my self.
I trust the inborn impulse to progress.

Two things are necessary for personal advancement, for spiritual and social growth. One is belief, firm faith that you will move forward; trust that the urges and the yeastings are your gifts that will help you rise in the way that is noble and right for you. The other is tolerant self-observation, full consciousness of yourself as you interact with others, as you play life's games, as you emote, as you make decisions, as you rejoice, despair, hope and act. Simply witness, without judgment, your life dance, accepting your present limitations with loving patience. You will gain a profound knowing and you will move beyond your bounds.

I am excited and enheartened when
someone puts energy into feedback for
me, even if I do not entirely agree.

When you surround yourself with loving people, it is possible to ask for fairly accurate reflections of how others see you and interpret your behavior. (You may even receive such valuable service without asking. Remember that you have the right to request a postponement if timing is off.) Know that you may choose what part of the images to accept and integrate with your concept of you. It is not necessary to accept or reject in the entirety. Look upon the whole offering as a marvelous gift. And congratulate yourself as you begin to receive less-than-favorable feedback without defensiveness — a milestone in the journey toward maturity.

MAY 1

*I accept a time of emptiness,
a fertile void.*

Do not panic at feelings of emptiness. Celebrate instead the priceless opportunity to take time for deciding, for self-acquaintance. Do not rush to occupy the hours, making commitments that may fill the void and foreclose the emerging new identity. There will be times of relative nothingness, no-thing-ness, space for the light of new meaning, moments good only for the touching of the spiritual essence of being alive. Relax; look about gently for fresh purpose. Explore patiently. Celebrate the opening in your life for exploring your rich inner landscape.

*I am ridding myself of the old beliefs
that have limited me. I believe
in the power of faith, hope, love
and the creative urge.*

You are ready to rise above any belief system that places you at the mercy of disease, ill fortune and powerlessness. Have faith in the probable healing effects of a healthy diet and exercise, of positive thinking, of loving so pure that it is a spiritual balm. Live in hope with visions and original plans for a future of peace and prosperity and adventure. Find bright new ways of sharing love with more people. Believe in the inner glow, the buried treasure in everyone and draw it forth with empathy and trust. Let love be your crystal ball. Use it to find the beauty others do not see.

*The people in my life are capable
of getting their needs met. I can trust
that they have vast reservoirs of
strength and competence.*

You are not capable of devastating anyone
as you go about constructing a life that suits
your sacred selfhood. Be unafraid of destroy-
ing any other. Only the other person can
destroy his or her own self. Taking yourself
out of a situation that harms or stifles you, or
significantly modifying conditions to allow for
more personal development, may call forth
capacities in everyone that might have re-
mained dormant in the past winter of your
self-sacrifice.

MAY 4

I am freeing myself of overattachments.

Overattachments are like addictions — you can never really get enough and withdrawal is painful. Overattachment to persons constitutes a kind of bondage for all involved. Addictions to security, sensations, status and power, things, places, beliefs and such require constant vigilance. You can never relax or you might lose some and then . . . the torment. Be attached, be involved, have preferences yet be ready to avoid suffering with a journey to your wellspring of inner power and peace and love. This center is a refuge and a place of true glory where you may return again and again in times of rejection, heartache and loss. Go there in still meditation, be there, be a dweller in a realm of deep wisdom and tranquility.

MAY 5

I will be ready to let go of something greatly desired and it very likely will come to me in greater abundance.

You cannot live fully in joy while grasping and trying too hard. Release yourself from such stress. Witness yourself in the struggle to gain or maintain something without which you feel life would be impossible or awful. Recognize such feelings as addictions. Reduce the addictions to preferences and pursue those shining goals with happiness and hope, relaxing in the possibility of not getting all you wish for. Become more comfortable with alternatives. Work for a new perspective, such as how your giving and receiving love fits in the overall picture. Refocus, redefine, readjust and do not be surprised if what you have been desiring comes rolling in when you have yielded graciously to other possibilities.

MAY 6

I am making my life a miracle.

There is so much opportunity for personal creation. You do have the strength to override bad habits, to rise above apathy and despair in constructive, creative action. That is truly miraculous. You also deserve a rest from time to time, which only serves to sweeten the miracle.

*There is much love and beauty in
the world. I am here to notice it, experience
it and add to it any way that I can.*

There is much in which to rejoice. There is
always purpose — simply adding to the store
of goodness, simply loving it all is noble
living.

Whenever you find yourself involved in
negative thought patterns, say to yourself,
"Stop!" and then positively affirm some aspect
of your world. Focus on the way sun and
shadow meet at the corner, instead of rehears-
ing dangerous "What if's . . ." before a meeting. Replay a friend's kind voice, the feel of a
hot shower or a puppy's rough tongue. Recall
something you have given, notice the song of
a bird and remember you do live in a wonderful world.

*My life is a meditation. I focus in loving
stillness on the beauty all around me.*

Quiet the apprehension, the anger, the
envy, the readiness to lock horns. As you walk
toward a destination; as you sit and wait; as
you run, dance, work, play or turn to fall
asleep — be in the presence of beauty and of
mystery. Notice the angle of sun and shadow
at the corner, fling open your hearing to
crickets and leaves, feel moonbright air on
your shoulder, raise your shades to even the
gleam of a star. Savor the flowers, the flavors,
cool grass on bare soles. Worship the touch of
one loved. Focus on lit faces and meditate on
life's most radiant smiles.

MAY 9

*I believe that anything wonderful
can happen anytime. I believe in miracles.*

Be ready for miracles or they may go
unnoticed. This requires a soft-set. Lives set in
concrete are not the best receivers for wonderful surprises. Begin to step out in new
directions. Act, knock on doors, notice when
they begin to open. See the beauty in the
beasts and there will automatically be more of
value in your life. Be as the photographer who
makes a masterpiece of the one gold leaf set
amidst a dark and gloomy day. Focus on the
golden leaves, find solace in the gentleness of
gloom and live among miracles every day.

MAY 10

I can add some joy to every day.

Do the unexpected. Break the habits. Go to bed early and rise before the sun. Be out where you may see the dawn's first glow. Be there when the sun is born again and again and again. And go to the river on Tuesday; search for animal tracks and other priceless treasures. Take a friend sometime and tell stories of childhood while you make boats from broad leaves and watch them sail away. Give gifts at the office. Ask someone to dance when your favorite tune is on the radio. Take risks, take joy, make joy — every day of your life.

I am a giver.
I am aware of the gifts I give.

You are a giver — if you have smiled, shared time or resources, listened without needing to blow your own horn . . . There are a multitude of gifts to be given — each one spreading ripples in ever-widening and overlapping circles of caring. Shine your light, sing your song, read your poem, show your shell collection, teach someone to hear a whip-poor-will. And if you do none of these, so much the better, for you may more likely find within or gather unto you some gifts the rest of us have never imagined. Give them valiantly. For the only shame is never to have offered from the heart.

*I have a loving center, full of
kindness, joy and peace.*

Only fears, jealousies and self-doubt separate you from that loving center. Do those
feelings seem like insurmountable barriers?
Try an unusual series of fasts — go one day
without being jealous or envious in any way;
simply interrupt with an internal "Stop!"
message. Try a day without fear, a day without
self-doubt or self-degradation of any kind.
What else separates you from your peaceful
center? Make such fasting a habit and see how
close you really are.

I need joy now. I take hold of the
possibilities of now —
the only immortal moment.

The past is only a scent in the wind; the future, a mirage. All that is real and lasting comes from the measure of energized cellular and spiritual self that experiences the present. It is good to learn from the past, to be aware of its effects. It is necessary to plan and take the future into account. But the result of failure to accept fully all that the moment offers is never to truly live. Do not miss the colors — *NOW*, the opportunities to touch and dance and sing and explore — *NOW*. Feel the smooth flow of ink when writing, respect the miracle of communication if you are reading, celebrate the ripple of muscles and the competent way you protect your back when you are lifting. Be wholly awake. Here, see, know what is going on at this time.

MAY 14

I celebrate my Earth-Self connection.

It becomes less and less comfortable to be ignorant of the glories of Mother Earth and Father Sun, especially as the bounty steadily vanishes. None can take it for granted. Your gratitude must grow each time spring does break through. Begin to celebrate those special times — drink a toast to the setting sun, the gathering rainclouds, the budding trees. Salute the mystery in the stars, recognize the brave struggles of the last heron on a dwindling stream. Touch more, smell more, see more, care more, wonder more. Enjoy more.

I can experience rapture in my life.

Do not settle for humdrum and hopeless. Reach out for the rapture. Know that you deserve the peak experiences that make life rich and radiant. Laughter is rapturous, shining, effervescent when it is pure and fun, not a put down to anyone. Look for the healthy humor and spread the belly laughs. Also spread a feast of new, wonderful experiences to share with special others. Use your imagination. Make gifts of the fresh crazy original ideas you have for *living* time (not *passing* time). Do a little research; find, combine, and co-create rituals and celebrations for a season or a day. Reach into a rich heritage of joyousness and make something exceptional happen for you and the ones you love.

My loneliness is lessened with every
wonder I investigate, with every
miracle I celebrate.

It is very difficult to feel lonely when you
are seeking answers, sifting through myster-
ies. Touch the green slickness of a new leaf,
run your fingers through living soil. Contem-
plate the message of a song, wonder at the
moods some music makes. Ask many questions. Answers are secondary. The searching is
the reason to live.

*I am continually reborn in the flight
of birds, the mystery and miracle of love.
I am vitally alive.*

Your vitality generates and regenerates. It
springs eternally from your spontaneous, fully
charged response to life. Do not be embarrassed at your energy, at the surges of excitement, at tears and shouts and acts of joy and
intense feeling. Uninhibited feeling and
expression of feeling in the presence of love
and wonder and reverence is what a strong
individual is all about.

MAY 18

*I am in union with the wonders
of the Earth.*

Find the place inside you where bird song
resonates. Allow the touch of rough bark on a
solid, rooted tree to ground you in serenity.
Take binoculars and wander with a turtle
among river reeds. Be wrapped in the silken
cloak of smooth spring air. You are no less
strong for loving the way a lizard crawls. You
need not climb a mountain to be fed at
Nature's youthful spring. Spill over with
daring drops at your next waterfall and feel a
union with the emerald pool below. Take
your heritage and preserve it, too — the one
planet of your birth.

*I accept the magnificence of this moment
fully, whether or not there is any
degree of certainty that such
moments will continue.*

Take full pleasure in the moment, even
though there are certainly no guarantees. For
what is a good life but a bright string of jewel-
like moments strung together on love and
purpose? The jewels are not any less bright
because there are gaps or possible breaks in
the string. Never negate a beautiful part of
your life. Validate all the good and excellent
parts — past, present and future.

I can be happy now; even though being
happy may not be exactly what
I thought it would be.

Happiness fantasies must be periodically
evaluated. Be sure that your definition is
reality-based and allow yourself to take joy in
what is available NOW. Now can still be quite
marvelous even if it does not nearly measure
up to future dreams. Be a fine detective,
ferreting out the best that can be realized in
the moments at hand. For character is also
built on sufficient satisfaction, not merely on
hardship. Besides now is the only time that is
ever fully real, the only time to truly be alive.

This ___(seed, leaf, spider spinning, etc.)___
is a miracle. I am uplifted in its presence.

Reach down; lift up a handful of rich, dark humus and worship the bits of miracle there. Do not miss the flash of light on bird wing in the setting sun. Feel the archness of a new highway overpass — know the poetry of its symmetry and strength, see it gleam like polished pewter in the morning sun and in its spirit see all the arches of the world. Be always lifted and flown in the presence of everyday magic.

*My choices arise from a personal
wellspring of goodness and wisdom.*

Be aware of the tendency to move from one
set of "should's" to another. Often we imagine ourselves free agents, only to find shackles
in the form of subscription to yet another rigid
value system or contrived perfectionistic self-
expectations in new directions. Notice when
you feel like you "should" be enjoying
something and you are not, when you are
driven to service because you think you
"should," when you are robbed of the joy in a
moment because you "should" be doing
something else or be operating at a higher
level.

Begin to function as a gentle self-witness
and to take confidently your own power over
choices.

*I accept fully the magnificence of what
I do have, regardless of anything
I have yet to acquire.*

A lack in one area of your life may be
legitimate cause for grief, but never for
discounting the value of other achievements,
relationships, skills, effectiveness, experiences or beloved possessions. Each one is a
treasure, no matter what else may not be
present now in your life. Stay in tune with the
abundance and more will surely come.

I can   (see, hear, smell, taste, feel, balance, . . .) . I am grateful. I use the senses I possess in fullness and great joy.

Pause several times a day for 30 seconds. Become quiet and calm. Tune into one of your senses. Practice acute observation wherever you are. Even though some of us may not have full possession of all senses, what we do have is very precious. Be filled with radiance in the gladness of these gifts.

I take great joy in relating to others,
even to those I am just beginning to know.
I let go of fear and the need to control
social situations and I watch hopefully
for beauty to emerge.

Return to the center, accept the challenge
of maintaining balance in social encounters. If
you are usually timid, try being first to draw
out the essence of another. Listen carefully
and respond to content or feelings with
further invitation to share. If you are most
often the leader, guiding and directing con-
versations in desirable directions, try letting
someone else be strong. Relax, maintain
gentle eye contact, allow yourself to be drawn
out for a change. If you are truly living in joy
at loving, your presence alone will urge the
sharing.

MAY 26

*I wrap the gift of my day with
remembrance of the bright spots.*

Take time to reflect in a quiet period.
Validate with your undivided attention the
parts of your day/evening that stand out
positively for you, that nurture your sense of
well-being. Often it may be the nonspectacu-
lar that spontaneously emerges, takes a bow
and smiles. Give it a hand. Make this a prayer
of thanksgiving.

*I claim the power in observation
and in wonder.*

When you are a wonderer, an involved, acute antenna — a loving observer — you become an active, integral and potent part of your world. Stay alert, play like a child and take it all in. Have you ever tossed from side to side the end of a hose running water? If you had, you would have observed that oscillation creates a spiral. Why? And why the thousands of convolutions on the underside of mushrooms? And how can woodpeckers stand to rap their heads all day? And how beautiful is the sunlight making rainbows in the hair of a friend! And how well you listen to her now — now that you are a powerful and observant discoverer!

*I offer a prayer to the morning
and I am renewed.*

Open a window or step out into the morning, early as you rise. Reach up to the sky, stretch tall. Breathe deeply. Feel the exhilaration of a fresh beginning.

Pray then to the morning, asking for its gifts so you may be full of joy and giving for the day.

O, bright morning, let me be as brisk today as your energetic, shining wind. Let me skip through this day jauntily, cheerily, as your dear chipping sparrows who fill every niche with their life.

*I offer a prayer to the night
and I am enriched.*

Allow yourself to know the night. Look outside, feel the air before bedtime. Receive a gift. Let a prayer to the night invoke the gifting, perhaps one like this:

O, velvet night, fill me with your peace. Allow me to relax a moment in the unknowing of your shadows as I must relax in the vast unknowing of my life, trusting in the wisdom of my inner guide and the rightness of the universe.

*I am aware of my progress through
the stages of forgiveness.*

Whether it's another person, yourself or
even life itself that you are forgiving, know
that there is no magic potion to swallow.
There is a process, a journey, a pilgrimage to
the blissful state of letting go. There is no
rushing. You may be moving through the
stages of denial, self-blame, feeling victimized, indignant and then proud to be a
survivor; and finally, feeling integrated and
more sure of where the hurt fits in your life.
The progress may seem very challenging,
slow, and frustrating. This road to wholeness
requires great courage and you are remark-
able in your willingness to move through the
pain and beyond it.

*I accept and celebrate the sweetness and
newness of this season of my time.*

There are new and wonderful things happening in your life. The trick is to recognize
them and give energy to their existence. They
are there, like the sprouting green grass
piercing warm mud after a gentle rain, like the
rose-colored blossoms promising fruit on
smooth brown twigs. They are there emerging, and a sharp eye spots them, just as an ear
tuned to song hears the first swallow of
summer.

JUNE 1

*I can create marvelous, multifaceted
experiences out of simple
acts of living.*

Eating an orange can be a trip. There is the
skin to begin, of lunar-landscaped terrain —
bumped and pitted individualistically, identi-
fiable as fingerprints. Inside reside sparkles
and squirts, fat nodules of fun. Bite down
slowly and tingle with tangy bursts of flavor
and fluid. Catch a subtle fragrance. Linger a
little longer with your small new world. What
else can you explore? What next on earth will
you discover?

*I am able to know and ask for what
I need from a listener. I communicate my
needs lovingly and respectfully.*

It is your right to ask for what you need.
You may need to be empathetically heard as
you ventilate and defuse strong feelings. You
may be unwilling to hear advice and feel
impatient with talking to one person after
another in a series of opinion polls. You may
simply want passive listening and a feeling of
support. You may need a quiet, warm hug.
Whatever it is you need or want, respect
everyone concerned by a willingness to
clearly state it with the understanding that
anyone has the right to decline. Consider also
the life-space of the potential listener and
communicate your gratitude for whatever is
offered.

JUNE 3

*I am more than any particular thing,
event, situation, behavior or characteristic.
I am an infinite being.*

You may feel totally wrapped up in some aspect of your life or your selfhood. It may seem impossible to separate from it. Spend some time in your inner sanctuary. Breathe the full circular breath — in deep and up, out and down. Come home for awhile to the exquisite whole organism that is yourself joined with all others in the vast biosphere, joined with the rest of us in the seeking-journey. Relax in kinship with all of us who hurt and search and rise again. Your silence grows like an expanding silver sphere and the gentle darkness of meditation flames with a spark of rising energy. You know that you are much more than any of the pieces of yourself and your life. You are always a miracle of consciousness and courage.

JUNE 4

*I am discovering who I uniquely am
and what only I can give.*

In consciousness, elevate your special
offerings to the level of unique contributions
to a universal cause. Center your breath, focus
on the essence of your present and potential
giving. What does it feel like inside? Where is
this sensing located in your body? What is the
shape and weight of it all? What is it all about?
What words finally come and seek to describe
this feeling? You have a special piece to fit in
the whole creative form. It is not like that of
anyone else because none of us fit into the
same mold. We are all unduplicated miracles.
Something good can come from you that can
come from no other. There is no doubt.

JUNE 5

*I know how to ask for attention
and encouragement.*

People sometimes forget to be generous.
We have much to do and to heal. There is no
shame in asking for your share of strokes and
recognition and understanding. Straightfor-
ward statements of what you need and desire
are often all that is required for a perfect
balance of give and take. You offer a priceless
lesson in loving when you respectfully ask in
good faith, trusting the integrity of the ones
with whom you share support in healthy
living.

JUNE 6

*I am kind. The kindness is a balm
and a wondrous comfort.*

Sometimes it is important to let go of
prickly feelings and urges to project them
onto others, especially when feeling frustrated. Be kind first to yourself, speak compassionately to your inner child, and then rise to
levels of reaching out in comforting ways.
Feel the healing power multiply.

JUNE 7

I share my values and increasing skill and
wisdom by demonstration and modeling.
I gladly give this important gift.

Guided by the star of your soul's wisdom
and the gathered light of your mind/body
intellect, you are moving beyond limitations.
There may be discouragement and lessons
hard to master, yet no accomplishment is
worth more than the transcendent expansive
life you are creating. Believe how vital is the
teaching you do by simply being in the world.

*I can be still and concentrate on another
person, fully honoring and appreciating
that individual's personhood.*

First, we must be quiet and touch center.
When the mind is rid of static restlessness, in
the heart is heard music — a melody of love.
The person with you is not an object of your
ego, someone to approve, protect or stimulate
you, but a real conscious sensitive being who
deserves your full attention and bountiful
encouragement. There is plenty to go around
and you will undoubtedly receive from the
pool of inspiration as well.

JUNE 9

*I calm my mind and perceive the ultimate
connectedness of all things.*

You are part of a vast and wondrous organism, the planet earth and the universe to which we belong. There is no system — geologic, biologic, meteorologic — from the minute to the most vast — that does not somehow connect to the rest. You are included. And your place is very precious, your loving heightened awareness vital to the health of the whole. You are welcome here and necessary.

I set realistic expectations for myself.
Step-by-step I accomplish and revise them.

Your potential is boundless and unlimited. Yet you dwell in current concrete situations with sets of skills and requirements for growth. Expectations set too low are insulting; too high and you invite failure. So set and keep a beat, stepping out in a rhythm of desire and achievement, in manageable segments until the dance drives itself and movement becomes fluid and free.

I live peacefully in the sea of life.
I am this sea as well.
I flow, flexible and fluid.

You are the ebb and the flow, the spinning diatoms, the mass of fish, the crystal waters, the path of spreading moonlight. You are at once unique and part of the completeness of the whole sea of being. You are an atom and the universe. Your oneness is as true as your aloneness. Always there is the vastness to which we all belong and sometimes it is good to relax and move with the tide, letting go, expanding . . .

*With these hands I have given,
received and created miracles.
I am grateful and proud.*

Look at your hands with loving appreciation. Have they stroked a frightened child,
held a bird with a broken wing, mended a toy
or a motor, kneaded bread dough, plucked a
flower for a friend? What ordinary, wonderful
acts have passed through your fingers? Let
them not pass unsung. Spend a moment in
reverence. Notice the love in your hands now
and watch the miracles they make tomorrow.

I celebrate beauty, talent, excellence.
In this way I join the dance.

If you see beauty, talent, love, accomplishment, expertise — excellence and fulfillment in any form, and if you wish to participate, celebrate it. Transform any energy-draining self-comparison or envy into acknowledgment of the burgeoning human ability to express and create in wondrous ways. You are part of this flow of magnificence, since all of us are joined in appreciation and joy. Release your own potential with fuller openness to all the best your human (and nonhuman) relatives have to offer. It is food for the soul and stimulus for your own creating.

*I carefully and joyfully appropriate
the gifts from my parents and
early role models.*

Like seeds in the waiting earth, gifts from
your parents and early teachers may lie latent
in your awakening self. Perhaps their positive
influence has already been shaping and
guiding you, yet not completely acknowledged. Perhaps resentments and frustrations
have kicked up an obscuring dust cloud. This
is the time to uncover the precious gems
given years ago and now a part of yourself.
What is the best you learned from them?
Recognize, celebrate and receive all over
again, this time in full gratitude.

JUNE 15

I am worth beauty and excellence
when I am alone.

You deserve the best, especially when you are alone. It is a powerful vote for high self-esteem to treat yourself with flowers, candle-light and good music, with a fire or a cuddle in a warm, colorful blanket, with a cooling dash through the sprinkler, with a bird feeder outside your window — whatever you can do to nourish and hold yourself dear. Create a garden of a sanctuary to return to. Each time you care for you, the message is received in the subconscious, "I am terrific. I am worthy of this goodness."

JUNE 16

*I am willing to seek and offer periodic
genuine quality human contact.*

Take inventory of your schedule and notice
how often you really connect with others.
Initiate time with people when you make
solid eye contact, listen empathically, share
genuinely, explore and experiment, celebrate
and have some fun. Seek such rich being with
many at various times, as no one person can
offer all you need to feel a deep sense of
belonging. Release stereotypes and remove
mental boundaries to this contact, for it may
be created in surprising places and a myriad
of ways. Be playful and enjoy more of your
earth-kin.

JUNE 17

*It is perfectly okay to be in low gear
some of the time. I accept my down time
as part of my natural rhythm.*

Pretending to be up is such an energy drain.
It is just fine to be however you are. There is
no right or wrong way; "should's" can set your
shoulders in concrete. Simply watch the flat or
low feelings, noticing patterns or possible
causes while letting it be — no negative
evaluation necessary. Without energy-deplet-
ing resistance or pretense, you will bounce
back sooner. Enjoy the break by allowing it to
be restful or by letting tears release some
tension. You are no less strong and much
more noble for giving yourself this time to be
just as you are.

JUNE 18

I now enjoy fully the rewards of the letting go and forgiving I have already accomplished.

You and your relationships thrive on whatever forgiving and releasing of negative buildup you have done. There may be subtle differences to notice and celebrate. A parent's birthday card to you may seem a bit warmer or more affirming. Your disappointment at perceived slights or attacks or neglect may be diminishing. You may already be expecting more miracles and finding them. You may have released yourself somewhat from the bonds of judgment and in so doing found yourself just smiling a little and accepting the once-irritating behavior of others that perhaps mirrored your own now-forgiven qualities and behaviors. Take notice of this and enjoy it all fully. You deserve it.

*My interest and excitement often increase
with deeper involvement in a project.*

It is difficult to predict at the threshold what
the country will be like upon exploring. The
desert, for example, seems barren at a glance,
yet reveals varied life forms, brilliant sunsets,
larks at sunrise and may even yield hidden
waterfalls and fern-lined pools at the base of
some far hill. Similarly you may find unlimited
sources of stimulation where you least expect
them, provided you program yourself to
remain open and expectant of zestful and
satisfying possibilities.

Once you have decided carefully on a
course of action, doubt and reduced enthusiasm may threaten your peace of mind. Be
ready. The void you feel at any one time may
be just the space you need for full creative
involvement later.

JUNE 20

I welcome opportunities to learn.

Whenever you feel emotional discomfort, life is offering a gift, an opportunity to learn. An associate who consistently arouses your defenses is presenting a mirror in which to look for your blind spots, to confront addictions, to see where healing and creative problem-solving is needed. Anyone who triggers your self-doubt, anger, frustration, sadness is teaching you how to be a better partner, worker, helper, creator, friend or self-supporter. The material is offered to you all the time for your selection. You create the curriculum and take the course at your own perfect pace.

JUNE 21

I freely choose my actions and responses.

Rigid or automatic reactions and responses to button-pushers are cues that some of your freedom has been eroded. Watch for tension or consistent negative judgment or other evidence that you are not flowing with the moment, ever-new to life, open and trusting of yourself and others. You may be rubber-banding, snapping back to old, out-dated feelings and coping mechanisms that no longer serve you well. You are fresh and blossoming in growth. Give each idea, person, event and situation a generous chance. Trust yourself to act appropriately, according to your unique values and abilities, your informed, creative and flexible awareness. You are the one who thus invites enrichment.

JUNE 22

I find balance in my sense of responsibility.

You need not say either yes or no without careful thought. There is middle ground and finding it requires releasing the need to be everything to everyone, to have total approval and admiration or control over all situations. All or nothing thinking can invite just that — overwhelming stress from trying to handle everything that may lead to illness, depression, burn-out or paralyzing fear of inadequacy. Give yourself the treat of checking out demands and expectations, especially of yourself. Are they realistic, desirable? Are you allowing others to be strong, too? Are you seeking love in your quest for self-perfection and super-person activity? Make a general rule to think about it for a selected period of time before committing.

*I find and welcome help when
I need extra motivation.*

At times all of us face hurdles that are insurmountable in solitude. Solo flying is fine unless the motor fades in midair or will not get us off the ground. Then it is desirable to ask for help, a boost, some loving motivation. Perhaps you could benefit from guidance in discovering what you want in this phase of your life. You may need planned support in taking that next step if you find yourself getting next to success and mysteriously backing off. You are wise enough to seek helpers and so your vital juices flow.

JUNE 24

*I am spending my time on what
is truly worthy.*

There is no situation that cannot be used to
make real your goals for becoming more
loving, effective, joyful and creative. Allow
nothing to be a waste of time. And begin to
carefully structure your life to allow the
accumulation of skills and understanding to
match your talents. Nurture the interests that
kindle your spirit.

JUNE 25

*I feel the urgency toward growth of
the summertime. I am energized
by the ripening of these days.*

You are deeply connected to the natural
rhythms and cycles of nature. The fullness of
the summer season — actualized growth and
prolific productivity of the earth, her gardens
and wild children — all move in your natural
self as well. You are part of it all and are able
to feel the life pulses quicken.

JUNE 26

*There is enough. There is plenty of beauty
and excellence in my world.*

Consciously put plenty in your life. Begin
with one thing, like the abundance of red in a
geranium, the new petals in a budding rose or
the musical millions of drums raindropping
on a tin roof. Create plenty of handshakes and
hugs, smiles and hot potato soup shared with
a friend. Bounty is built, one red geranium at
a time.

*I am discovering what good relationships
are all about. I deserve to be treated
well and to be highly satisfied.*

You are increasingly decisional about
relationships. You are becoming more aware
of your deep loyalty to yourself and of options
for dissolving ties that do not contribute
consistently to your well-being. You may
choose to remain appropriately loyal at a
particular time if the other is very ill or going
through a terrible stage, yet it is essential to
protect yourself and to see that your needs are
met until the situation is resolved and you can
move on to fuller living. And when you
remain involved, do it with as much genuine
love and caring as possible, having made the
decision consciously to do so, for masked
negativity is no help at all.

I take an expansive look at my life.
I seek and find a broad vision of myself
and my life direction.

Sometimes we must step back and ask, "Where do I want to be in five or ten years? What do I want to be doing?" Allow this question to simply be the focus of meditation or free form drawing or a flow of natural writing. Program yourself to allow the subconscious and the Higher Self to speak through dreams and images and intuitive heartfelt interests and urges. Give yourself plenty of time. Seek guidance, if you feel stuck, yet play in the whole thing as if it were the grandest adventure — this designing of a dynamic, purposeful life.

JUNE 29

I am able to delay some gratification for long-term gains. I find a variety of sources of satisfaction along the way.

Reaching for the high note — a distant goal — need not have all or nothing overtones. Build in sources of gratification, create a reward system for yourself, seek the inherent joy in every task and situation, make more meaning from your over-all sense of high purpose. The journey is also beautiful with sunsets and surprises. Watch for them. Receive the blessings. On your way to some greater state of being, you will find that you have already arrived.

JUNE 30

*I am effective at taking just the right
amount of time to examine a course of
action, considering the implications
and possible consequences.*

It is of utmost importance that we delay
what may be impulsive action long enough to
look at possible outcomes and a variety of
alternatives. Much stress, grief and loss of
control can thus be avoided. Excessive rumi-
nating on a decision can also block your
potency. Therefore balance is of the essence.
Seek help, professional or otherwise, to buy
some time for consideration, for relaxed
contemplation and information-gathering
away from the heat of emotion and in the
presence of someone who will encourage a
step back for the big picture. Keep two or
three phone numbers handy for calling in the
thick of compulsive tension or when tempted
to decide while on a high.

*I am realistic about how much energy
I put into a relationship and what I
receive from the arrangement to increase
the love and joy in my life.*

Initially, you may have invested a great deal
of energy in a relationship. A state out-of-
balance does not last long and your needs,
perhaps even your partial withdrawal, may
create a vacuum of nurture and creative
loving. Expect a miracle, however. Allow for
clear communication, nonjudgment and
patience to work their magic. At the same time
become increasingly clear about your needs
and your desires for a healthy, balanced
partnership. Become accustomed to claiming
this for your total health and to seeking
alternatives for bringing such mutual support
into your life.

*I treat myself with kindness
and compassion.*

You are not giving yourself permission to
be lazy, but are simply maintaining alert
attention to your awakening, even in times of
impatience or deep discouragement. You may
feel like an imposter, just pretending to be
successful, or feel too paralyzed with negative
interpretations of reality to begin the journey
you know will be long. Give yourself a break.
Be kind and award yourself ample credit for a
list of everything you accomplish each day
toward your healing and growing. List the
subtle things, like allowing some anger or
tears without shame, or taking time for a
stretch in the sun. Even the act of making the
list could be listed, especially the attention
you are giving to your blossoming love for the
core self that is you.

*I awaken the inner witness and ascend
to simple observance of internal
states. I am letting go.*

With the disinvolvement of the observer
self from the body, feelings and ideas, there
comes an energizing freedom. Without active
attempts to repress, resist or exert control, an
attitude of noticing and letting be allows more
awareness and you will notice leaps of insight.
More emotional competence will happen
naturally. Accepting and nonjudging, your
inner manager grasps at nothing nor pushes,
yet eventually holds all in a loving heart-mind.

JULY 4

*I invite others to share the sense of
purpose I have about my life.
I support and celebrate theirs.*

Give some thought and initiative to sharing
the process of creating and energizing purpose with one or more supportive people on
a regular basis. Give strength to one another
as you share your purpose statements, as you
share the essence of your most positive selves.
Offer one another unconditional support as
you explore the difficulties of purposeful
living and celebrate enthusiastically the
successes. Consider including others who live
far away by writing letters. Widen the circle.

JULY 5

I am a zestful, sensual being.
This is my birthright and I claim it
with lightness and courage.

The great kindness you offer your precious body-self includes a loving, giving attitude toward the innocent, playful self who desires opportunities to delight in the senses. Give the gift of smells that you enjoy — perhaps cedar incense or sandalwood, roses, cinnamon tea, a favorite cologne. Offer yourself long hot baths with oil to create smooth, supple skin. Feel the aliveness in ripples of muscle while working out and in languid stretching when you are done. Dance free-form in your private rooms; open your arms to sunshine in the park. Live in your body now. Lighten up with the self-evaluation. It is time for you to claim this joy and add to the freedom consciousness for all of us.

*I am open to intuition, trusting this real
and holistic way of knowing.*

The key to developing intuition is maintaining a peaceful alert awareness, even in the stormy inner world of feelings and ideas and agitation. Willfully interfering reduces receptivity, so be still.

Practice focusing on that spaciousness. Close your eyes while you sit relaxed in a safe place. Attend to each sensation for several moments and then move to the next. Feel your eyelids growing heavy on your cheeks and attend finally to the space within your forehead. Feel it grow, remain and expand with it. In the quiet, your antennas are ready to receive like a finely tuned "dish" on a clear, starry night. You carry this readiness with you.

I am learning how to give to myself. I give myself permission to change old images and messages and to enjoy my unlimited potential.

You are becoming enlightened, first softly and then brightly glowing with health, radiant with the effects of your kind self-care. You are expanding your realm of choices, acknowledging points of active decision in response to situations, people and relative to your own plans. You recognize your rights to energetically meet personal needs, to feel whatever you feel, to first be loyal to your well-being, to release responsibility for the problems and feelings of others. You are honestly examining reactions that indicate snapping back to old familiar response patterns and belief systems. You are stepping out into the sunlight, a free child of a bright universe.

*I notice the perfect unfolding
of those I love.*

One of life's most precious surprises is the
miraculous recognition of virtue in just the
way someone is, right now, no requirements
necessary nor pressure to change. Suddenly,
with a shift in the perceiver's expectation,
beauty and perfection are revealed. And, of
course, growth accelerates in the presence of
such holy loving.

JULY 9

I am proud of my ability to accomplish and to structure my life while developing spontaneous playfulness.

Many ancient sources of wisdom deliver the delightful message, "Lighten up!" It is tempting to continue taking ourselves very seriously at all times. That is no longer necessary. It is highly desirable to get silly sometimes and to play with abandon. You are moving into a perfect balance of humor and seriousness, business and pleasure, structure and free-for-all. Perfect for now, that is. The balance will sooner or later shift its center of gravity, so be ready to roll. (Try it, really — rolling. Roll on your bed, down a grassy hill, across the carpet, over a layer of crisp, fall leaves . . .). Lightly. Take it lightly.

*It is good to let others be in charge
at times, to share the responsibility and the
opportunity. I welcome the relief
and the enrichment.*

When you let go of some control, the results may not be exactly as your own orchestration would produce. You may initially feel uncomfortable, but it is vital to your well-being to share both the burdens and the glory. You will feel more secure and relaxed in the long run, as you find yourself reprioritizing time and energy with less need to keep everything and everyone in order by yourself. Communicate clearly your goal of balancing output and management. Be patient. And practice frequent uncontrolled behavior, like strolling, following the whims of your partner, not your plan. You may receive the gift of newness and adventure.

I can be flexible and relaxed while identifying the power I have in my life.

When you know that you do have power to shape your hour, your day, your life, you can be naturally less rigid and more at ease. You need not try to relax.

Identify each day several options that you have and note whether you elect to exercise your right to actively decide. Expand this honest inventory to a week, a month. Anticipate choices a year, five years from now. Start small, with your choice of extra morning sleep time or time to meditate or sit and sip a cup of something or see the sun come up. What else? Feel pride in your growing appreciation of alternatives. Notice how peaceful you become and how much less need you have to control yourself and others.

*I observe gently, watching for evidence of
black-and-white thinking. I frequently free
myself and stand clear, filled with peace
and a release of energy.*

There is such a roller-coaster of feeling
associated with black-and-white thinking. You
may want to contract with one or two others
to gently help you notice this tendency to see
all or nothing. Watch for evidence yourself,
such as feeling like you can and should do
everything when your energy is high and
feeling like nothing is possible or worth the
effort when you are down. Notice it (or
celebrate its absence). Do not try to change
anything. Just be aware. Watch for swings of
mood and reality interpretation. Accept
responsibility for either seeing yourself or
others as wonderful or awful.

I am opening up to feelings. I increase my capacity to attend with confidence.

You can attend to feelings, observing an expanded consciousness. You are letting go of resistance, attachment, fear of being overwhelmed. It is a result of gradually "disidentifying" with the feelings — you are not the feelings, nor are they permanent. Crying does not make any of us weaklings; neither does anger equal uncontrollable meanness. When we try neither to hold on to positive feelings nor to get rid of uncomfortable ones, it becomes clear that all emotions are transitory. Even deep depression which seems interminable can and will end. Highs do not last forever. Change is the first law of nature. There is such a release of energy when, watchful and loving, you let the feelings flow through.

JULY 14

*I am accountable for what I realistically
affect in my environment, allowing
others the right to their own responsibility.*

Be awake, alert and observant daily, in the
interest of balancing your sense of responsibility. Notice when you feel guilty or responsible for something largely out of human
control or for which control is better shared
among many or is the choice of someone over
whom you have little real influence (as a child
over a parent's self-destructive behavior).
Take note and release any behavior that saps
energy. Check gently into the past and say
good-bye to guilt for what you could not have
changed. Create a right responsibility ceremony and claim only your own.

*I take all the time I need to fully
appreciate and absorb the positive
energy I receive.*

You are brave and courageous and wise for
choosing the path of healing, of greater self-
knowledge, wisdom and expansion. It is not
easy to keep going, to take up again and again
the cup of purification, the challenge of
reaching fullest selfhood. You deserve encouragement in whatever form it comes your
way — compliments, smiles, a warm touch, a
look of recognition and acknowledgment,
expressions of gratitude . . . Open up and
receive the good, collect the treasure and let
the sweet rain soak in.

I recognize my kinship with all in the universe and feel the easing of relationship needs.

No one person or particular kind of love is necessary to your happiness as you realize your relatedness to everyone and everything. As you open to the kinship, you hear the sameness, see the similarities, know we are all in this together, regardless of exteriors. You have only to claim your place as sister or brother — not more, not less than any of us who also strive and rise and fall and rise again. Even the garden spider, whose web the wind destroys, is our relative — one who spins and spins again in beauty to live and to thrive.

*I am harmonious and peaceful in the
presence of others, able to intuitively
experience their highest being.*

Your composure, born of the quiet, centered breath, places you in the unique position of tranquility in relationship. Less agitation and approval-seeking behavior, reduced
judgment and added focus on the interior
beauty of others results naturally in genuine
encounter. In the still, fertile moment, insight
flourishes, intuitive perception penetrates
fast-fading barriers. There is harmony of heart
and spirit, and so two or more know the
perfection we all share.

The love inside me flows out easily.

Tender, affectionate feelings well up, filling your heart more often. It is more comfortable for you to widen and extend the stream bed of emotion and let the love flow effortlessly. More of life and fellows and universe are cherished everyday. This internal treasure increases and cannot help but move outward. In your own way, in your own time, at your own rate, you open the floodgates and send forth the nourishing waters of devotion to all life.

*I am becoming a person who attracts
a great deal of love.*

You are now drawing to you the ones who
can honor and revere your specialness, who
hold your well-being dear. As you are learning
to do this more for yourself, you are becoming luminous with release of energy and
wonder and faith in you, in others, in the
universe. Such being is magnetic and vitally
appealing. Those who want the same gravitate
toward you and share the miracle of mutual
empowerment.

*I see myself whole and thriving
in relationships.*

The image of yourself as successful in relationships grows with each affirmation of your worth and love-ability. In the growing consciousness of abundance, you can recognize the value in every relationship, ultimately claiming expansion and enlightenment. You are accumulating tolerance, acceptance and multiplying your capacity for unconditional love. Others will bloom in the springtime of this giving. Even the ending of an intense phase of relationship becomes liberating as you perceive freedom to join in refreshing new ones. As communication is open and honest, respect is deep and expectation positive, satisfaction gathers in your deserving heart.

JULY 21

I am a unique and precious person.

You are emerging perfectly from the personal, priceless design within. There is no one who can be in the world the way you can. You are part of the wondrous variety that spices and enriches our world. You direct the unfolding with your growing trust in the inner voice. There is no telling what riches of personhood are yet to be revealed.

*I am learning to take care of myself
with gentleness and commitment.*

The kindness in your eyes is first for you.
Tender, gracious and benevolent with yourself, you turn from within to embrace the
world with mercy and profound respect. Your
earnest engagement in honoring the pledge
to well-being, your high search, your continu-
ing journey of healing and development is
rewarded in each meaningful *now* and often
bursts forth with joy.

*I can choose to see myself in
a beautiful new image.*

You are a vast and uncharted universe, a
being of unknown dimensions. Old limits no
longer apply. The images and expectations,
the "should's" and even some values of the
past may be dissolving in mist, out of which
will rise a new creature. This is the mythic
dream — a sleeping one kissed and awak-
ened; in this case, touched by the healing self
and transformed with fresh promise. This is
your story now.

I acknowledge the vital presence,
worth and potential of others.
I am one who empowers.

As you are more able to see yourself whole, you are able to offer healing and empowerment to others. Your own emerging High Self recognizes the great human possibilities in others. We are all capable of this and though we may not be in this space at all times, once having experienced it, we are awed and enchanted by the beauty of it. The glimpses of profound possibility stay with us. So with your own healing rises the ability to look into another, to offer your own eyes for the seeing of dynamic potential underneath masks and postures. To be acknowledged by another, at any time, particularly in times of pain, confusion and discouragement, is to be gifted.

JULY 25

*It is healthy for me to laugh
heartily out loud.*

If you laugh lustily, bravo. If you are
developing this talent, be encouraged by
medical reports of happy effects on the
immune system. Laughter begets laughter and
even someone who might judge you harshly
is probably moved somewhere off a stuck
point. Your healthy laughter invites others to
abandon real or imagined cultural bondage
and have fun. If the laughter is at no one's
expense, humor is a high gift. Our chuckles,
squeals and guffaws mean that we have
simply been gracious enough to receive.

JULY 26

*Beauty shines through me. I am becoming
a manifestation of infinite life, love
and radiant power at work in the world.*

You are a microcosm of universal life force,
love and consciousness of beauty and creativity. You are increasingly able to heal yourself
and spark the healing motivation in others.
Your power flourishes with your ability to
create value out of challenging situations. You
are functioning better and better, using a
fuller range of potential. You are choosing to
become a miracle. And it is happening.

*I allow inflow of joy from
unanticipated sources.*

Your qualifications for enjoyment are
changing, becoming more flexible. There is
more perceived beauty on a grey thundery
day, more inspiration in brief encounters with
a variety of people and beings, fewer requirements and less need for particular, exotic or
spectacular origins of satisfaction. More often
experiences of previously doubtful value
yield serendipitous rewards. Relaxing the
resistance, you open up to possibilities never
before imagined.

JULY 28

*I am involved in a healthy
exchange of energy.*

There is inflow and outflow. There is
balance in peaceful acceptance of both
responsibility and abundance. You are noticing the effects of behavior changes that create
such balance. You are becoming adept at
going beyond the fear and sending your
energy out in bold and healthy new ways. The
return is often beyond output, yielding a net
gain for giving and for reinvesting in the
building up of a reservoir of vital life force.
Where the exchange is consistently or heavily
unbalanced, you are aware and able to move
toward equilibrium. Even this is a ripple of
good sent out into a learning, evolving world.

I, —————*—————, *am caring, playful,
intelligent and in love with the world.*

(* *Include your name for
greater power of affirmation.*)

This affirmation may or may not fit your
exact personal needs. Write one for yourself
that reflects the characteristics you sense
within and would like to enhance. Use the
above as a model, unless you identify with it
at a deep individual level. You are such a
priceless being. Join with us in the dance of
co-creation. Constantly affirm the highest and
best in yourself and accept all that you
perceive. Use it all for the making of the
miraculous life that is your sacred right.

It is okay for me to feel confused about priorities. I am learning who I am.

There is no time limit on the discovery of self. You may still feel hazy about clarifying your over-all goals and setting priorities. You may feel that the time for fuzziness and confusion should be past or that you should experience no recurrent conflict. You may expect clarity now. It is certainly all right to want it now and to have your feelings of disappointment or impatience, but give yourself the kindness of accepting where you are, continually learning about yourself and your options. Your patience may be taxed, and yet you can relax in the knowing that all beings unfold in their own way. Panic-action reaps sad rewards and you are worth all the precious time it takes to find sweet clarity.

*I choose to see myself as a winner,
regardless of the outcome of my decisions.*

You really cannot lose if you see the world
as a place of opportunity for growing and
learning, regardless of the path chosen. If you
focus immediately on the winner-either-way
model, gather adequate information, establish
priorities and trust your heart's urging, your
chances are excellent of being happy with a
choice. Even engaging in the process of aware
informed decision-making means you are a
success.

AUGUST 1

*I claim the real power in admitting
exactly where I am.*

There is immense muscle in honesty, the
kind of honesty that over-rides pretense,
denial or other defenses. When you can
acknowledge accurately where you are, having cultivated acute self-observation skills
with a noncritical eye, you can open to help of
all kinds. Resources are recognized. It is easier
to say, "I need help. I need other people. I
need input." Your energy is free to flow out
and your integrity magnetically attracts the
good.

AUGUST 2

In the reservoir of my stillness is immense power. The power is within me.

In the essentially still water lies potential energy. When released, there is life, work, productivity. Your silent, still knowing is the home of an empowering spirit. This silence is pure power. In this stillness lies great strength. It may not be immediately realized, but keep going to the well. It will be known and claimed.

I breathe into myself. I breathe into my centered, loving self. I am the loving center and from here I go forth.

Going forth from this space is a gift to all. From this space flows the courage to be fully yourself, to smile and encourage, to move beyond fear in fulfillment of your potential. From here you move more freely, to touch, to listen, to share. From here you most genuinely encounter life.

I have accomplished something important today.

Take generous inventory. There is at least one significant thing you have done today, probably many more. You may be surprised at how important a simple act may have been for someone else. Your list may include the reading you are doing right now. In fact, if you are committed to finding meaning in all situations, every aware moment or moment recreated in conscious-awareness is of consequence. Give yourself full credit for each precious effort.

AUGUST 5

*I, _____*_____, have the power to
overcome my inertia today and to reach
out to people, do good work
and experience joy.*

(Include your name for greater power
of affirmation.)*

You are a storehouse of potential with a
reservoir of energy for fuller being in the
world. No matter how latent this potential
energy may seem at any one time, it does
exist. You have the power to release it, to
make the noble choice of taking positive
action. The outreach will energize you and joy
will be incoming from unexpected sources,
including your own flowing spirit.

On the way, enacting my purpose, I notice that means and ends are the same.

We all have a reason for being here, although it may seem buried, like a precious jewel, a bright, sparkling starlike diamond in the rough. When this universal purpose — high guide to your yearning, striving, giving — is discovered and brought forth and daily acknowledged, goals become clarified and means for reaching them are no longer separate from the whole. All is part of the perfectly complete process. Pursual is constant, achievement is infinite, moment to moment, when you are dedicated to your purpose. Everything fits.

*I consciously choose when to ventilate
and more often I am comfortably quiet,
joyful, creative or processing constructively.*

You are moving toward the center point,
the perfect still place within. Being quiet here
does not mean holding anything in with
discomfort. It is not part of the complaining. It
is beyond the self-indulgence of prolonged
depression. It is meditation in the midst of
communication. It is here that your spirit
grows strong.

AUGUST 8

*Whatever I choose, I give my
healthy best to it.*

Your healthy best requires balance —
equality of respect for yourself, others and the
project, whatever it is. It means not rigidity or
compulsive overwork, but commitment,
careful planning, enthusiasm and self-care. It
also requires flexibility and permission to be
outrageous, spontaneous and playful as part
of your plan. Your best is only as good as your
whole health. You are coming ever nearer to
this perfect balance.

I am free to be myself as I grow and experiment. I am having fun.

When we give up trying to impress everyone, the journey is much more fun. So from the basically sound floor of your own self-respect, you can try more comfortably to experiment in fresh arenas, even enjoy a chosen old behavior pattern that fits just fine for now. Take a step back, smile at yourself and invite a spirit of lightness and fun to join you.

In a challenging situation, I relax and then do what I know how to do.

Sometimes the toaster is just not plugged in, a screw is loose on the doorbell, the batteries are dead. We have learned to examine mechanical devices, see how they work to some degree, making the necessary adjustments, before and after cursing them. We learn finally to look first, do what we know to do and find that we save a lot of headaches that way. This is also true of life's challenges that you may perceive as unfixable problems or even as disasters. Accept what you cannot change about a situation only after you have calmly examined the problem and the possibilities for taking some constructive action. If sought creatively in love and acceptance of all concerned, desired results are often remarkably easy to achieve.

*I am finding out and acting on
what works for me.*

The only really helpful basis for choosing
behavior is whether or not it works to make
you feel good about who you uniquely are.
Basing choices on external approval is like
perching on a precipice. The wind can blow
you either way. Settle down into the center of
yourself and in the protection of your own
healing thoughts, notice and record what
works and keep it going. The energy output
will decrease, as this healthy system infinitely
feeds itself.

*I am caring and helpful and I am
responsible only for my own life.*

The illusion is that we can actually change
the lives of others. Actually, we can bring our
love and best efforts, offer our highest selves
with minimal effect on someone else. People
are choicemakers. Offer in full awareness of
the power of their own choices and with no
addictive attachments to particular outcomes.
Give as your heart leads you to give. If the
choice of the other is to receive and to use for
healing and growing, rejoice. Meanwhile, live
your own life in peace in every way possible.
Expect those miracles and model the attraction of abundance.

*I am responsible for the effects
on me of others' behavior.
In this I have great authority.*

You are not automatically hurt by the words
or behaviors of anyone. You may choose to
feel hurt by the way you perceive the words or
actions, your understanding of where they
originate and why. The reaction may be out of
awareness and seem to support simple exter-
nally imposed cause and effect. Imagine the
effect of perceiving someone you know
looking right at you and ignoring you. You
might interpret that behavior as a slight to
your personhood and feel upset. However, if
you discovered that she had suffered a
temporary sight loss, no effect on your
personhood would be created. Such an
example is, of course, simplified, yet we can
never know or fully appreciate the complexi-
ties that motivate others.

I am loose and relaxed.
My body feels free and easy.

Whatever you are doing, there are parts of you that can be loose and flexible. If your hand squeezes the pen, your jaw and shoulders and hips need not be tense. When you stand and move, imagine the muscles flowing with energy, not bunching up. Consciously relax the bowel for fuller elimination. Let your neck muscles just melt like butter in the warm sun. Allow your arms to swing loose, shoulders down and soft when you walk. Your body deserves frequent kindness.

*I grow more and more comfortable
with transparency.*

You may choose to share or not to share
any particular piece of information at any
particular time. This holding is most healthily
done in honor of timeliness or appropriate-
ness, not out of fear. The mode of secrecy or
hiding something can be given up, surren-
dered. It may have been useful in the past.
Now openness and a more satisfying relationship is called for. Believing in total acceptance
of yourself and others and giving that, you
attract it as well. With all of your material,
revealed or not, you are wonderful, just the
way you are.

AUGUST 16

*I look back only to receive gifts and to
release. I am committed to living
fully now and to moving with
purpose on my journey.*

There is nothing to be gained from dwelling of the past without a plan. Purposefully release guilt and resentment. Release the energy held with that as you would a captive bird who longs to soar in the sunshine. Purposefully sift through the old material for gifts — opportunities to become very wise; for unrecognized positive influences, values and qualities that you are glad about. Look also for patterns of behavior that you may be repeating in the present. Look with awe and gratitude. But do not look for too long at once. Know that ultimately your only focus will be on *now.*

*My quietude passes through everything
with love, carrying melodies of atoms,
breath of stones, songs of earth and stars.*

Times of mental quiet are priceless. In
those moments we can hear, feel, align
ourselves with the rhythms of Mother Earth.
Whether sitting still or climbing at-one with
the mountain, the restless chatter ceases and
there is boundless communion.

A bubble of joy arises.
I allow it to expand.

In the ocean of consciousness, bubbles of joy float up. Protect them with your concentration before they break on the surface of the sea. Fill that bubble with your attention until it spreads and finally dissolves its bounds and becomes the sea, becomes you, becomes all there is in the perfect moment.

AUGUST 19

*I gladly retire to silence and meditation
the moment I feel restless or disturbed.
Calmness is restored.*

Follow the breath to a place of inner quiet.
Let those agitations settle down, down, like a
smooth lake clearing. Ask yourself and others
for time out. Take the time in honor of
growing peace in the world, as it begins with
each of us. Fill your heart with the peace of
meditation and pour out hearts full of it for
the thirsty souls around you.

AUGUST 20

I need less and receive more.

Be aware of needy feelings, near-panic at
not having, unhappy comparisons of what-
you-have to what-others-have. These are
opportunities to reduce addictions to the
level of preferences. These are gifts —
occasions of awareness to be with; time to
focus on, perhaps even to share, something
you *do* have, to be reverent about the presence in the world of something you value
(whether or not you possess it). It is a chance
to be quiet and to achieve peace in a crunch.
Often such an attitude attracts unexpected
good.

*I am reawakening, reclaiming the
wide-eyed wonder of a joyful child.*

Every one of your cells sparkles with
eagerness to embrace the world of wonder.
Your countless mouths of molecules hunger
for cool nights under the stars, following
Jupiter and Mars as they travel across the dark
and brilliant sky. Watching a spider weave,
listening for crickets after sunset, hearing the
rain with a friend, learning something fascinating and new, experiencing the miracle of a
good hug — the simplicity and utter magnificence rekindles your youthful fire.

*I am clearing out, cleaning house,
winnowing the wheat. I keep the treasures,
the spaciousness, the golden grain
to nourish me.*

You are blowing off the chaff, dumping the debris, having sifted through for keepers. You are learning and letting go. You are called by flowers, bright skies, birdsong and laughter. There are rich and fertile fields to play among. You are claiming the gifts of your past and your right to peace. It feels you like a fresh fragrance, a clean wind, a nourishing harvest of joy.

AUGUST 23

*I accept the perfect gifts and opportunities
to learn in every situation.*

A situation may seem far from the ideal, yet
it is perfect in that it offers feedback about
what you may need to release in order to
grow. Of course, in this sense, it is you who is
perfect for this time in your life — perfect in
your willingness and ability to participate
consciously in the process of learning by
living.

*I am intentional about committed
relationships.*

As you become more able to give and
receive love, more open to deep and satisfying relationships of all kinds, you will find it
easy to be drawn toward high profile involvement. Be intentional and purposeful about
promises. You need not be too free with your
promises, implied or stated, to be perceived
as loving and supportive. You do not have the
energy, the personal resources to support
many in tangible ways. However, you can
support everyone on a level of acting out the
universal principles of unconditional acceptance and recognition of their highest purpose.

I perceive abundance in many forms.

You are a deserving recipient of never-ending gifts. Give yourself permission to receive. For example, if you are at leisure or alone when you would rather be working or with someone, focus not on the lack but on the opportunities — opportunities to feel leaves crackle under your feet as you walk, or to catch your breath at a swirl of golden leaves on the wind, to see the green of new buds, catch a whiff of roses, listen an hour to a bird song, write an old friend who is far away. Attend to the Bounty, whatever form it takes, for it is a shape-shifter and you will be often in glad surprise.

*I make my life so inspirational that
others voluntarily learn from me.*

Pressure and advice or teacher behavior
usually closes down the very ones you would
open to the truth. Let your example shine with
so much light that no one can miss the good
at work in your living. What you are is the
finest gift you have to give and others gravitate
naturally to learn about your success. So the
work you do on yourself is ultimately for us
all. We are community; your happiness adds
to us all.

*I recognize the role of commitment
in success and achievement.*

When we perceive a failure in life, it is often
not completely so. However, there certainly
are less successful situations where the key
missing ingredient was full commitment, total
investment of intention. You cannot fool your
whole organism wise-self. If you waver on the
fence regarding the worthiness of it all,
consciously or subconsciously, the endeavor
is undermined to some degree. Trust your
intuitive knowings about what is right for you
and wholeheartedly commit. Greater success
is assured. All things work together for this;
your energy flows, you miss no open doors.

239

AUGUST 28

*I acknowledge the parts of past endeavors
or relationships that were good or
left unexpected benefits.*

There are no total losses. If you feel a sense
of failure, it may help to take careful inventory. Leave no good uncelebrated. The enjoyment of any time of life is to be congratulated.
It is not easy. The successful completion of
any aspect of production or service is worthy
of recognition. And celebrate, too, what you
have learned about yourself, the opportunities
you have had to forgive, the depth of life understanding you have gained. Now, you are
totally successful as you move in any fashion
on this road, carrying with you only the most
select and useful bundles of memory and
treasure.

*I attend to my chosen priorities
and they are magnified.*

Make a list of what you want in your life. Be very selective about what to attend to now. Prioritize and turn the bright golden laser-beam of your whole spirit and mind on the priorities. Watch them expand, filling your world. Lament none of the unchosen. They will have a time when the breath of your love and your work will fill them. For now, keep your positive focus, concentrate and build your ideal world, a new structure, beyond the illusion of scarcity. You are a potent creator.

AUGUST 30

*I give myself credit for whatever
I accomplish.*

Your accomplishments are yours alone, excellent as they stand, not in relationship to an ideal or to someone else's. Do not discard a feeling of success for doing something because you think anyone can do it. You are unique. The forces that shaped you are unique. Your situation is special. This is true for all of us. We each own every one of our accomplishments — large and small. You finally got your desk or closet organized; you did some stretching this morning and felt less groggy; you planned realistically and completed a task. Whatever it is — give it a hand.

*I communicate and request support
in meeting the challenges of
overcoming old habits.*

You know the value of openly talking it out,
of asking for help and for feedback when you
have a habit to overcome, such as over-
reaction. If this reaction pattern threatens the
well-being of a relationship or the people
involved, a cooperative effort is often essential. Be aware initially of behavior and feeling
and perhaps of their roots. Thank them for
their past usefulness and bid them good-bye.
Let go. Then ask for gentle reminders from
your partner as it again occurs. Defensiveness
will fade away in time and you can receive the
feedback with gratitude and full knowledge of
helpful intent, cooperatively growing in love.

I enjoy demonstrating my good feelings.
It is a gift to all.

Follow joyfully your intuitive urges to demonstrate your love, your joy, your excitement, whatever positive feelings well up. Let them spill over and nurture you and those near you. Go ahead, dance a little in the grocery aisle, hug someone spontaneously, give a shoulder rub, break into song — even off-key. Give a gift without thinking about it, as if the gift gave itself. This is the give-away path. The attention and energy enhance and enlarge the good.

My giving is boundless and creative.

Release limitations on your giving. When you freely choose, giving can nourish you, even when you feel needy or empty. The giving fills you. It links you to all. For example, if on your birthday you are feeling let down, call or write someone whose birthday you forgot. Offer support and caring now. Set a date for more contact. Give gifts in honor of your birth and in gratitude for the opportunity to create your life now. Allow the form of the giving to vary. The shape may change even as you offer. Your needs and the needs of the receiver are the loom on which the gift is woven, a loom that itself changes in the act of creation. Be open to the shifting, creative act. Be open and humbly receive, in turn, from those who have honored you with the taking of your blessing.

I am capable of setting up situations to nurture myself, to meet my basic needs and beyond.

You know what you need to remain healthy and happy. You arrange to share hugs and conversation, to exercise in the open air, to plant your feet on Mother Earth, to eat nutritious food, to learn and expand your mind, to hear music that nourishes your soul. So many things can lift you. You know what you need in your life and each day you become more adept at putting it there. You find the resources, seek them out, offer thanks and return the goodness full circle.

SEPTEMBER 4

*I am aware of the potency of loving
touch for health. I seek and
give loving touch.*

Full hugs, massage, holding hands, a touch
on the back, a stroke of the hair — all send
messages to the cells, who sing, "We are alive!
We remain devoted to the health and life of
this being! Praise be!" Seek and offer the
magic touch; it turns our lives into better than
gold.

*I can intervene lovingly and remain
unattached to any particular outcome.
I am independent of the outcome.*

You can offer an intervention or feedback
or confront behavior in ways that respect the
readiness and receptiveness of others. Seldom
is anyone able to hear you when they are
highly emotional or feeling overwhelmed. Be
supportive, present or out of the way, wait for
a better time, come from a space of unconditional caring and be willing to accept that this
still may not be the time for change. Each
person requires varying amounts of time to
learn the lessons of a situation. Keep loving,
offering, developing communication skills
and making your own life a miracle.

I am in charge of my own life.
I take responsibility for filling my life
with what nourishes my health
and happiness.

You are adding, adding, adding so much that is positive in your life that there is less and less room for anything negative. The winds of your positive focus fill the sails and you are moving powerfully and gracefully now on the sea of all being. You belong here. You have embarked on a voyage of great importance and great promise.

I accept my feelings all the time.
I go on bravely.

The feeling part of yourself has a high and sacred right to your unconditional love and acceptance at all times. Your feelings are your feelings. They simply are, no right or wrong. Ventilate, ask often for support, for holding and touching in your feeling time. Ask the nurturing parent part of yourself to gently allow the expression. Some times are hard and you will pass through. Refocus as soon as possible on the behaviors that set up your success. Return again and again to the temple that is your daily heroic life, bringing offerings of all the good things you know to bring into your reality for your well-being.

*I continue to develop competence and
beyond in what I choose to offer the world.*

You need not be perfect or extraordinary or
even good at whatever it is that you choose to
do as your work-gift. Continue to grow
towards excellence and keep doing it, giving
along the way. If you are not doing yet what
you would choose on a full-time basis, be
glad for the opportunity to prepare for it and
to offer what you can whenever you see a
chance. Celebrate and operate at the highest
level possible at the time. Be grateful to
yourself for the courage to let be as is, for
letting it go into the world.

*I am a master artist, creating my
own picture of the real world.*

You choose the canvas, the colors, all the
tools of creation. What will you paint? It is
yours to do. For example, a man may be
working around a pool in a beautiful naturally
landscaped area. Those relaxing there may
experience his presence as a rebuke of their
laziness, feel sorry for him and guilty for their
own leisure, or perhaps perceive an intrusion
on their privacy. The same people can also
see him as one who has a job, is therefore self-
sufficient and who is working in a pleasant
environment, helping maintain the beauty all
enjoy. Good feelings abound in the latter
scene and cordial exchanges may enhance
goodwill all around. We each paint a little
piece of the universal picture, and each piece
is a reflection of the whole.

I am willing to pay some prices, make some trades on my way to fuller satisfaction. I honor my choicemaking.

Something may have to slide for a while. Eventually your wants and needs and your resources will all come together and be in perfect balance. If that is not yet so, be patient. You may need to focus resources and energy, kindly setting aside some things for now — activities, ideas, projects, material acquisitions, whatever. You may have to put away the tables to make a space to dance if the dance is that important to you. You may mourn the tables, yes, and the apparent unfairness of it. And let them go. Grow peaceful with this in your own time.

SEPTEMBER 11

*I am responsible for efficiently
creating space for good feelings.*

Accept the feelings of doubt and anxiety
with far vision, know that they pass and that
witnessing them patiently facilitates the
passing. Fears and fatigue, loneliness and
frustration visit us all, yet it is possible to
shorten the duration. Give these visitors as
little reaction as possible. Ask for gifts of
understanding only. Do not give them so
much attention that they feel invited to stay.
Watch for self-punishment; it will leave, too, if
you know the game. Consequently there will
be so much more room to create the presence
of sweeter things in your life. Gradually there
is gathered a joyful crowd, leaving little room
for anything else.

I give myself time to build a fine life.

Everyone feels impatient at times. Acknowledge the "hurry-ups" for what they are — old internal tapes that can be turned off. Hastiness is often costly and you need all your resources to build a temple, a cathedral, a majestic structure — your life. Breathe slowly, relax, get in touch with the impatience. Accept the feeling, explore, recognize the value there and then set it out. Transform impatient feelings; explode them like fireworks in the darkness of an imaginary sky — a celebration of your willingness to take all the time you need.

*My life is a cycle. There is no end without
a beginning, no ebb without a flow.
I patiently experience the natural rhythms
for I am part of the world.*

You are never really "there." Be at peace
with the truth in that, and know your life
continually seeks balance as nature does.
There is reaching out and pulling in, outflowing with gifts and receptivity, darkness and
light, winter and summer. The seasons of
being will not be pushed. Your unique cycles
of dying and clearing, planting and waiting for
the rain, blooming, bearing and harvesting
will never end, but will start over and over
again with seeds in ready ground.

I give it all up and freely open my heart.
I am enriched beyond all measure.

Give up the neediness, the craving, the fear of insufficiency. Breathe through it. Be motionless, touching center. Believe in the miracle of openness and unrestrained giving to others. When the sharing arises as a joyful expression of your creativity, not as "duty," not for reward, you are simply acting out your basic reason for being here on earth — to love yourself and your fellow beings.

*I unconditionally love and respect the
child within me, no matter what.*

The needs and desires of your beloved
inner child are so precious. They have helped
you survive and retain a vital core of being
that refuses to be contained in falsehood and
artificial restraints. This child has longings that
are the stars in mountain lakes and wind-
dancing flowers, the tree-climbing, the bare
feet in mud, the hugs and hideaways on
summer afternoons. The fears of this child
must be heard and considered. The pain of
this child deserves attention for healing. The
wisdom of this child can bring you back to
truth. The spontaneous play of this child is a
gift to the universe and from all the children
whose heritage we preserve with our bodies,
our full expression of self and archetypal joy
at bonding with the earth.

SEPTEMBER 16

*I seek and find people in my life
to model living in love and community.
I add my positive life force to theirs.*

We all need models for help in structuring
new more satisfying lifeways. Include these
teachers in your vision of glorious living and
attract them with your desire and attention to
following the path of harmony. Witness any
resistance, pass through it and learn. Thus the
wellspring of your wisdom and experience
and gratitude swells and overflows — a gently
trickling stream, a geyser at times, a nourishing reservoir always. You model and teach as
well. The circle never ends.

I have incredible courage. I am proud of how far I have come with vision, willpower and persistence.

You have much to be proud of. You have survived and are programming yourself for high well-being. The spark of divinity within you leaps up when you recognize how admirable you are and what a miracle you are making. You fashion that miracle even when you feel stuck. Old patterns are being continually rearranged. In every moment subtle shifts occur and the transformation is more complete.

SEPTEMBER 18

There is magic in my life.
I believe in the power of my positive
self-programming.

Each conscious choice of constructive thinking and being is an incantation, an invocation of the power to move the mountains that have seemed so impassable before. The obstacles begin to dissolve, the shapes of things shift and change, what seemed to be issues before are no longer perceived as problems. Your belief in this process and your commitment to it is magic.

I am merciful with myself.

Even when pulling yourself out of a tangle, be as kind and merciful to yourself as you would be to anyone else. You are so much more encouraging to others when you have lifted your eyes to the highest vision of yourself. Lift them again and again and rise to it.

*I am continually learning. I am glad
to practice my new skills in the vast and
wondrous laboratory of my life.*

You have been given all the equipment you
need to experiment, to learn, to create magic
in your life. Be ready for the extraordinary
chemistry of your newly emerging self com-
bined with the validating and vital elements
you invite into your life. You are catalyzed
into new being everyday simply because you
are willing to do the necessary work. And
since means and ends are essentially the
same, the work is already the joy that you
seek.

SEPTEMBER 21

*I am connected to the movement of
the planet. I feel the balance
of the autumn time.*

Autumnal equinox marks a golden time of
equilibrium on earth when all is poised in
readiness for change. Times of inner balance
allow us to gather strength, as the mouse
gathers seeds and the bear gathers girth for
safe passage through the winter. Feel the
wisdom of this balancing, gathering for
yourself all you need to pass through. Join the
quickening, enlivened by golden afternoons
and brilliant flashes of colored leaves. Join the
quieting as harvesting is done and the earth
waits, ready. Balance the quickening and
quieting; the work, the rest; the brilliance and
simple bareness, like the trees.

SEPTEMBER 22

*I focus lovingly on someone to whom
I have not recently offered support.*

Every loving thought increases your love-ability. Focusing your thoughts, your energy, your deepest felt sense of loving and good wishes on one person for a period of time opens vast reaches of the soul. You may not notice it all at once, for the effects accumulate as you regularly practice "blessing time."

SEPTEMBER 23

*I accept the challenging parts of a
course of action with courage.*

Do not be surprised when there are times
of painful challenge, of apparent blockage.
There may be times on the way to a goal when
you feel sad or doubtful or overwhelmed. Let
the tears flow or scream at a stop light
(windows up!). Ask someone to just listen, to
hold you, to nurture you. Release some of it if
it builds up; let go. Relax, recenter, and move
on boldly.

*I deserve to receive and to give the vital
elements of excellent relationship.*

You deserve the best. Giving is a privilege.
You deserve the give and take of the essentials
of healthy relating — unconditional acceptance and respect; maintenance of each individual's wholeness; empathy and understanding; genuine concern and support of one
another's well-being; trust and honesty;
willingness to communicate openly; consideration; some shared interests, attitudes and
beliefs; tolerance of differences. It is supreme-
ly worthwhile to spend time and energy
examining and strengthening these aspects, to
contract with partners for mutual attention to
them. It is important. And stay light in it; be
full of wonder at the magic of it all.

I consciously join in community with others to build and maintain all our highest self-esteem. This is a joyful, creative effort.

We are all part of a vital human community. All members of the community are partly responsible for the self-esteem of others, including our own at various times. Your part in this human family project begins with unconditional acceptance of all persons in your life, with the suspension of harsh judgment and negative criticism. This is bedrock and may take years to develop. Accepting yourself as well, allow the celebration of progress in this endeavor, eliminating self-punishment. As you expand this loving attitude, your presence in the world will be felt as nurturing. Other attributes will follow — increasing and deepening feelings of love.

I carefully plan activities that make me a whole, interested, interesting person.

You are a multi-faceted person, interested in a number of things. Invite more of these interests to emerge. Even if you schedule just one a month, conscientiously plan activities that have nothing to do with your work or your usual routine. You are much more than that. You are increasingly becoming an expansive person who is vitally connected to many life dimensions.

SEPTEMBER 27

*I become light and easy-going, fully
able to enjoy the life interests and
explorations I pursue.*

Remember to "lighten up" and not take
yourself too seriously in any of the endeavors
you choose, especially your work. No matter
how important the activity or responsibility,
you are not it. You are more than any one
aspect of your life, more than the sum of any
combination. The more variety you add, the
more you know how adaptable you are and
how deep runs your core self. You are an
infinite being, a miracle beyond measure, no
matter what. So, plan something special for
you — today. Stay light and be fun.

*I am able to develop closeness
and intimacy.*

No one develops healthy relationships
without a willingness to work at it. It is not
easy, yet it can be joyful. Even in the midst of
challenge, there is joy if you remember the
beauty of what you are about. Growing close
and letting each other in is like journeying
into a vast and exciting new country, for each
of us is a whole, incredible world. You are
perfectly capable of maintaining your own
equilibrium and of carefully determining the
degree of sharing you are willing to do right
now. You are in charge of yourself, yet willing
to let flow, willing to take the steps toward
intimacy that will give wings to your life's
journey.

With every breath I draw in the precious
life force. It surrounds me always.
I draw it in now.

Your breath is the catalyst of your living.
Imagine that a force field surrounds you and
that it is composed of white light. Allow the
breath that sparks the sacred life within you to
be carried in with the light. If you are fearful
or agitated in any way, remember. Remember,
too, when you feel fine. Draw it inside and
remember your connection to all of us who
breathe this holy way.

*I am authentically myself. I am who I am,
and I love all of me now.
I trust my growth and my being.*

There may be times when you feel far from your ideal. You may feel very judgmental, for example, and have difficulty accepting yourself and others, perhaps much more than you would like. The only way to move beyond all this is to love yourself even in the unloving. And when you cannot do that, relax and let it be. Be quiet with it, recognize it and then do something constructive or fun or peaceful or helpful. Perhaps the behavior will be your opening door. And if you feel stuck and cannot act, simply witness the stuckness and all that goes with it. Just watch. You are already a miracle, complete in this moment, just the way you are.

OCTOBER 1

*I focus on one or two major projects
at a time. I let others go
gracefully for now.*

Save yourself from dis-stress. Allow yourself
to fall within present limits of wholesome
striving. There are always many worthy endeavors. You cannot do it all at once. There
will be a time for the other things. Relax and
focus and enjoy what now you choose to do.

OCTOBER 2

*I am perfectly fine even when someone
is angry or disapproves of me.
I am basically competent, capable and
loveable. This fact endures.*

There may be a tendency to panic, fearing
rejection or abandonment when someone
disapproves or ventilates impatience or anger.
Do not dismay; breathe into your deepest
center. You are okay. Often you are not the
target. You can handle the situation, learn
from it and grow. Nobly, you come from your
greatest self and you are strong.

OCTOBER 3

I can relax and rest peacefully.
I allow space to just be.

It is perfectly okay to be nonproductive and un-busy at times. In fact, it is wholesome and desirable to schedule do-nothing time regularly. Gather some special smooth stones. Keep one with you and sit with it in your hand from time to time. Feel its weight and temperature, feel its substance in your hand. Feel its history. It links you to the earth from whence you come and to which you belong. Rub the smooth rock between your fingers, tumble it in your palm. Watch your thoughts rise and float away. Have similar connecting experiences near a tree or watching clouds out of your window. Perhaps there will be no thoughts of connecting or doing anything. It is good to just be, perfect being.

OCTOBER 4

I am having more and more fun.
My playfulness increases the
joy level all around me.

Now or very soon will be the perfect time to become more playful. Some of us played little as children or repressed the child-self later, and may need others to help us now — to initiate, to encourage letting go. The child in you can be released into the sunlight, can learn to abandon care and have outrageous, wonderful fun. Laughter keeps us young and healthy, so actively seek people and places to help yourself play.

*I keep careful account of the elements vital
to my goals. I am well-organized.*

There are always choices of activity. It may
be necessary from time to time to withdraw
from some ritualized activity that seems
necessary, but which could be occasionally
skipped in order to get better organized. You
will be more relaxed and more fully able to
concentrate. Your effectiveness and enjoyment will increase beyond measure.

*I have goals. I have a vision. I can focus
and patiently move ahead.*

Commit your goals to paper, to memory, to
frequent visualization. See yourself where you
want to be, doing what you want to be doing.
Feel the feelings, as you are functioning at
your highest level and your fullest capacity.
Commit completely and be willing to set
some other things aside for awhile. Know that
there will be some delayed gratification, yet
less than you may think because you are
capable of making the journey joyful. Stick to
it, brave warrior. If it should seem too constantly burdensome, make no emotional
moves and seek help deciding to change or
carry through. Whatever you decide, you are
blessed as a person of conscious, visionary
living.

*I know how to achieve an appropriate level
of healthy stimulation in my life.*

You know yourself very well. You know
how much stimulation you need in order to
function at your highest level. You are a
unique individual — you may need more or
less music or movement or travel or conversation or learning than someone else. Notice
quickly your subtle warnings — early signs of
restlessness or depression. Set up your adven-
tures or your quality time alone. Say yes to life
and to whatever *you* need for renewal, youth
and vigor.

OCTOBER 8

*I can choose a different interpretation
of a situation.*

Whatever is going on in your life, there are
various ways of perceiving it. You can set up
your scope from a different overlook and seek
another view of the whole thing. You can
wear rose-colored glasses or dark gloomy
lenses or clear ones, letting in the light of
acceptance and love and greater creativity.
You can choose your own ways of seeing it all.

OCTOBER 9

*I accept my sadness, my anger and
my impatience. It passes.*

Sometimes the challenges seem overwhelming and perceived injustice is a heavy
load. Feel what you feel. Know it will pass.
And remember the power of your self-talk.
You are a master internal story-teller. No one
view of reality is exclusive of others. You may
see things differently later. For now, the
feelings are fine.

I create a vision of excellent living.

Often we compare our lives and ourselves
unkindly to a myth we have called normal. We
may think of ourselves as below normal or
wonder what normal families are like. Some
of us can never measure up to romantic views
that vastly transcend our present reality. Most
likely, neither can anyone else. Embrace the
part of this that is visionary. Love your
yearning for more. Choose wisely the most
realistically satisfying, yet transcendent desires
and mold it all into a high vision, a guiding
star. Join us all as we create the future, beyond
all romanticism, real and grounded in skillful
living and loving.

*I learn from all creatures. I accept guidance
from the positive symbolic qualities to
be found throughout the animal kingdom.*

Have you recently watched a spider spinning her web? She is patient and organized.
She trusts her inner knowings, swinging on
the wind from branch to branch, dropping her
strong silver lines behind. She paces herself
and intuitively spirals out and in, creating
from within her own body-mind-self an
inspirational structure that catches the last
golden rays of sun.

The spider is a legendary figure of creative
power, who symbolizes cosmic order. She is a
weaver of the senses, creator of life. She is a
sun symbol, her threads created within, as are
the sun's rays. She is the weaver and the web
itself, just as we are. She models the creative
self and we are her pupils.

I am planting seeds, leaving behind a legacy for the future. This brings me great satisfaction and joins me with the human family in harmony.

You may not literally be planting maple trees for the grandchildren's syrup, but you are leaving behind traces of yourself. Every smile, every creation, every bit of support you offer, every story you tell, song you teach, lesson you share is a seed for the garden you are making of life, a kernel of the truth you are living. It all makes a difference, so continue the sowing. Only the future knows the harvest.

I believe in myself. I encourage others and let them know that I believe in them.

Recognize the high value of encouragement. In our lives there are those who have faith in us and because they do, we are survivors. Search your memory for those who have trusted in your worth, who have treated you with respect or given you special attention, validating your potential. Some are obvious, others more subtle, with effects no less vital. We all work together in community to add to one another's capacity for knowing at some deep stratum of pysche — "I believe in me." Continue to surround yourself with those who willingly give and receive loving mutual support.

*I accept and use well the precious energy
from support and encouragement.*

Identify and be with some people you can accept, respect and trust. Make a decision to suspend disbelief and allow the sweet energizing effects of positive strokes to be felt. Let the energy sink in as if through all pores and into every cell, becoming thoroughly internalized. Trust that your wise organism will accept that which is good for you. Feel the aliveness, the quickening and know it will be used for something wonderful. Already it is bringing you — a precious being — more joy.

*I spend my energy wisely on preparation,
and so I am ready, full of
life and confidence.*

Self-confidence springs from adequate preparation for a task. Worrying is a waste of time. Visualize yourself doing and being just as you would like, fully competent and complete. Spot the areas you need to develop in reality. Begin right away, stay in the moment, doing what you know to do right now, each step leading to the next. Do not be surprised at success. Claim it and be suffused with satisfaction. You deserve it.

*I reverently and patiently recognize the
importance of learning to accept
myself and others just the way we are.
I am learning at just the right pace for me.*

We have the perfect amount of time — a
lifetime — to learn how to release ourselves
and others from the psychic solitary confine-
ment of criticalness. Judgment imprisons all
of us. Only when we let go of the need to
control with our evaluation and the conse-
quential flow or restriction of love, can we
truly connect with anyone, including the
essence of the self. So relax, loosen your jaw.
Notice what is. Give many positive strokes,
put chips in the bank of self-esteem. State
your needs if you must — simple, non-
directive, non-punitive, straight messages of
your perceived requirements. Be patient.

OCTOBER 17

*I offer what we all need and so I
open the way for feelings of
connection and kinship.*

You may feel needy at times. Reach out
from that and give, for it is likely that someone
else needs what you need. We all require
many of the same things — positive recognition of our existence, validation of our
strengths and successes, understanding,
affirmation of our worth, a kind and listening
ear, help with the big hurdles, quality time
with friends, caring, closeness. When you
offer those things to anyone, you reduce your
isolation and the loneliness of us all. We are
all related in our need for love and our ability
to give it. You are no exception. You are an
incredibly able giver of love. It is your human
birth-gift, this programming for loving.

OCTOBER 18

I increase my connectedness. I reach out every day to someone.

Initiate daily bridging of the gaps between us. Let someone know you a little more; get to know her or him better. Take the risks slowly; you need not be effusive or become transparent overnight. Gently, gradually lower the drawbridge and invite some special people in. Eventually the castle walls will dissolve and you will dwell in the comfortable cottage of your warm and welcoming heart. It is time for you to claim this peace, for it is your birthright and it is waiting for you.

OCTOBER 19

*I offer my partners in relationship what
every being deserves. I am real,
generous, accepting and caring.*

Mutual attention to the elements of a
healthy relationship is essential, regardless of
the depth or nature of the relationship. A fully
satisfying relationship includes people who
are willing to see and be seen realistically.
This requires an attitude of sincere mutual
acceptance — of self and one another just the
way you are. Then from the basis of honesty
and real respect (not fantasy), relationship
can grow in all other ways. You care enough
now to be authentic and to validate the
perfection in the imperfection, to let it be
okay however each one is now. Thus you lay
the foundation for the warm bonding to build.

*I consciously practice ways to lift
myself and bravely move on.*

You know the behaviors and thought
patterns that can lift you right out of discouragement. It may be dancing around the house
to a favorite piece of music, working on a gift
for a friend, calling some folks you have not
reached out to lately with your love. You may
need to speak firmly to your hand, saying,
"Pick up the phone." You may need to keep
the art supplies handy or the dance tape on
"Play" because the difficulty is in beginning.
You begin and the rest follows. Celebrate the
energy and ride it to more constructive
behavior. It spawns, births and feeds itself,
and can be reseeded again and again.

*I have the right to care for myself,
putting myself in the best possible
situations for my well-being.*

You have a sacred responsibility to take
yourself out of harmful situations. Productive
life roles do not require prolonged discomfort. You are valuable in our community of
awakening beings. You deserve to be well
cared for by the wisest self within you. You
deserve to find and pursue that which brings
you satisfaction. You deserve to love and be
loved, to use your body and mind fully, to feel
the wings of your spirit unfurl. Put few
qualifiers on these unfoldings. Invite the
healthiest happenings and allow surprises.

I cherish glimpses of the vision.

It may seem that the curtains part too seldom. You may be ready for all to be cleared away — the insecurity, the fear, the envy, anxiety and loneliness. Be assured that as you continue your search, you are learning, you are evolving, sometimes gradually, other times with bursts of speed. One day the curtains will remain parted and light will pour in steadily for longer and longer periods. Meanwhile receive the light in even the briefest instant of revelation. It becomes part of you, no matter how long the timeless moments last.

OCTOBER 23

*I am receptive to the wisdom
and strength of others.*

You cannot know it all, nor would you want
to. A most marvelous gift is the kind of
receiving from another that validates his or
her personal potency and wisdom. The truest
masters instill in others the sense that each
one is infinitely wise and valuable and
capable. People seek to be with others who
invoke their strength and talent. This is the
greatest giving.

*I meditate on the gifts of circumstances
and more of life is desirable.*

You are finding that circumstances over which you have no control are less threatening as you creatively interpret them. The phone company's mistake may give you a quiet evening with a good book. Perhaps your strong desires to have telephone service restored can be transformed into appreciation of those you call and time spent updating your personal directory. Required fasting before a medical exam could be cause for frustration and complaint. On the other hand, it could be an opportunity to examine compulsive eating habits or to structure time in some new ways, like singing instead of snacking.

*I hold myself dear. I give and receive
abundant support and so I come
from a ground of confidence.*

In times of conflict, we are so much more centered and calm when there is plenty of support, rather than scarcity. Setting up that support is one way of loving yourself. It is easier to rise above habits of panic and over-reaction when no one is the only one. A wide support system is an incomparable life resource that allows the courage to be who you are, to stabilize and become masterful at creating loving, mutually nurturing relationships of all kinds. And with acceptance of this truth comes more and more awareness of various sources of support, opportunities for connection. The search itself is a door to the treasure.

OCTOBER 26

I am alert, communicative and cooperative, creating new freedom in relationships.

You can be free of old unhappy patterns of relating. You will be much less likely to over-react, to fear rejection and abandonment if you are well-prepared. Remain awake, alert to the self-talk, the automatic interpretations, the habitual behavior patterns that threaten the health of the relationship, such as panic at confrontation. Notice and take five. Have an internal pep talk ready. Then communicate your desire to cooperate in rising above this. Ask for gentle reminders; have a back-up behavior system rehearsed, such as an affirmation to prevent defensiveness or a response that invites explorative dialogue. Be inventive!

OCTOBER 27

*I am increasingly relaxed about life and
my reactions are more and more
appropriate to the circumstances.*

There is a trick to serenity and appropriate
levels of life drama. The trick is a variety of
meditation — focusing on the solar plexus
and calling up the Old Wise Self within. Be
with this powerful teacher for 30 seconds. You
may have an image or a name for this being.
You know all there is to know already. This
focusing method simply allows access. You
are infinitely wise and knowing. Tranquility is
your birthright and you are claiming it.

*My emotions are a natural part of
myself. I feel, accept, express
appropriately and release.*

Emotion is a natural form of expression, a
natural human capacity. It is energy moving in
the body. Sometimes it is appropriate to
outwardly express emotion, not to hold it in.
Often the tension of holding in is dangerous
to internal organs and to all body systems.
You are capable of finding and creating ways
to express that are not harmful to others or to
yourself. No emotion is good or bad, although
some may feel better than others. All feel
better, more healing and empowering when
the energy moves and does not stick, accumulating residue. The ultimate in emotional
control is not to stop having any, but to let
feeling flow and then let it go.

*I simplify my living and so am in tune
with the natural order of the world.*

Much of the tension in our lives results
from over-complexity. We are bombarded
with information, requirements and con-
sumer stimulation. "Get more, go more, do
more," creates over-stress. It is time to
simplify, to return to the natural rhythms of
the earth, to get in touch with a force that runs
deep and high and wide and runs also in our
veins when we are still. The force is felt in
green and growing things, in wonder at the
phases of the moon, in the flames of a camp-
fire, in a warm hug and a listening friend. It is
found in silence, in falling rain, in the turning
leaves of autumn. It is found in you.

Limitless is the possibility for a
wealth of experience.

You have plenty of time for more experiencing and knowing and loving than you can presently imagine. Regardless of how much time of living you think you may have left, it is all you need to live fully. Recall many of the things you would love to do. Instead of bemoaning the possibility of missing out on some — all of us will miss some — allow the loving of the list to energize you. Start with one to concentrate on now, the one closest at hand and move on it. Ask for help; receive it graciously. Believe the other things are possible and take steps in the direction of the next. Keep believing, keep moving, keep on highly living.

OCTOBER 31

I remain in the moment.
The moments flow.

There is no other real time but now. The past is a memory, the future yet to be. If you miss now, you are missing life. Take life in its entirety. Do not miss the little girl's story, do not miss the sparrows filling the bushes as you wait for the bus or the tire repair. Concentrate, meditate on the task at hand, be it drying a dish or designing a mall. Let each motion, each fired nerve-ending relay the baton, from one full moment to the next, of your earth-nurturing purpose, your dream that happens *now.*

*I have all the time I need right now.
I am relaxed and ready.*

You have all the time you need to do
exactly what you want and need to do. Each
moment has infinite potential for full concentration and efficiency. Any projecting back-
ward into "I should have . . ." or forward into
"I don't know if I can . . ." is a colossal waste
of that potential. There is clock time and
subjective time. You can by slowly releasing
tension and then trusting the flow, make any
amount of time all that you need to experience and learn and create and play and work
at your peak.

I am committed to making real my dream.

Take plenty of time to refine and nurture your major dream. Some pruning may be required or deeper planting in the ground. Some fantasies may need to be stored away with blessings for now, while the more reality-centered aspects are given power to transcend. This power comes from your total commitment to the dream. Even if you cannot work on it full time, your unwavering vision and affirmation and regularly scheduled quantities of time and energy are given. Negative thoughts are changed and constant steps are taken. When there is absolutely no wavering, no "Do I or don't I?" powerloss, the universe will provide in many ways. So start on your way, get the word out to others who might be supportive, show your dedication and expect miracles!

NOVEMBER 3

*I am patient with my progress
at positive thinking.*

Be patient with yourself. You are moving
along beautifully. You may notice yourself
back at the same old place again and again.
However, you are spiraling upward, perhaps
coming back around yet always at higher
levels of consciousness. You cannot slip back
in consciousness — sometimes in behavior,
but not in awareness. The doors have opened.
The spiral dance is yours. Rejoice in it!

I choose my activities freely.
I relax into them and act with noble
calm and enjoyment.

Even if they do not seem very attractive or you have not yet explored in other dimensions, there *are* other options besides the present behavior you have chosen. So whatever you are doing, do it in full awareness of your choice and if you decide to continue, do so without resisting or withholding, without resentment or tightness. Let flow your curiosity, your compassion, your kindness, your unique ways of experiencing humor and playfulness, your ways of moving into a state of peaceful strength — whatever adds honor and goodness for you right now.

*I eat consciously. My eating habits
are healthier and healthier.*

Our food choices today include more
healthy foods, including fresh produce, whole
grains, quantities of pure water, juices and
herb teas. It is well-known now that what we
put into our minds *and* our bodies largely
creates who we are. A diet high in processed
foods, refined sugar and flour, saturated fats
and oils, colas, caffeine and other drugs may
seem to give you normal energy, yet is worse
than insufficient for sustained high perform-
ance and excellent health. Such substances
can make you groggy, headachy, moody. You
are wise to confront addictions and to purify,
simplify. Take in purer food with a blessing, a
moment of quiet and gratitude. Relax. Affirm
that the food will be all your body needs to be
at its very best. Affirm the same for that
occasional hot dog as well.

Parts of my world are mirrors of myself.
I notice compassionately the reflections
and changes that follow.

If there is a great deal of hassle in your life, there may be a great deal of internal struggle going on. If there is external hostility or pain or rejection, these conditions may reflect similar internal affairs. Witnessing this inner-outer connection is a good way to know yourself better. If there is lack in your life, ask, "What am I withholding?" Begin crowding out the resentments and other undesirables with generosity and gifts of listening and kindness and playfulness and joy. One moment at a time, one piece at a time, refurnish the temple of yourself and watch your world change.

NOVEMBER 7

*I accept the gift of some discomfort
and so I learn.*

Discomfort or pain of any kind is an
indication of being alive. It is a form of
communication to your mind-body system. It
could be letting you know that some changes
may be needed for the sake of your wellness.
It may also be affirming that you are presently
meeting challenges and stretching beyond
limits. It is not to be agitated over, but to be
respectfully heard and heeded.

*I offer gratitude and ask a blessing as
I receive food. I am more fully
nourished than ever before.*

As you chew a bite of apple between your
teeth, give thanks to that apple and the tree
from which it came; remember the growers,
the pickers, the water and sun and soil that
nourished it all. Say to the apple, "Your
nourishment shall sing in my body; in every
one of my cells your life will move. I am
grateful."

*I deserve to be nurtured and cared
for by my surroundings. I deserve
a personal sanctuary.*

You need a place. Create in your mind an
imaginary place that is restful and safe and
pleasing to you. Follow your breath there
often and enjoy. Know that the essence of that
place can be created in your external world,
too. Your home, a room, a corner, a window-
sill with an arrangement of pine cones and a
photograph — a place to be regularly where
you can experience who you are fully and
where good, calm feelings are evoked. You
deserve it.

*I am the universe. All things are
contained within me and I am a part
of the wholeness of all being.*

Our bodies share the same elements, the
basic building blocks, as do the earth, the
trees, the stars. In fact, the elements were
forged long ago in the hearts of ancient stars.
We share feelings and behavior patterns and
learnings and longings with creatures and
human beings from out of all our planet's
time. There is no way you are alone. You are
part of everything and it is all part of you.

NOVEMBER 11

*My joy increases without bounds as
I surrender judgment and practice
unconditional loving right now.*

Every person you meet is worthy of the
transformation of your criticalness. No one
really needs it. It rarely helps and is especially
damaging to yourself. More useful and happy
is the look in your eyes that says, "I believe in
you."

*I find and gather to myself supportive
people who accept me as I am right now
and freely uphold my growth.*

We are not designed for isolation. Especially when handling a challenging relationship or work situation or life passage, join or
gather a group for sharing and mutual support. It is soul-nurturing to help others have
what they long for, to give extra life force to
their purpose and to be with them in the
making real of dreams. Their support of your
journey, in your way and your own time,
allows the filling of your cup and the over-
flowing in all other areas of your life.

NOVEMBER 13

*I am feeling forgiveness and
unconditional love and support in a
challenging relationship.*

We all experience relationships that challenge our capacity to fully accept and uphold
the other just as she or he is. Even if that
relationship is with a tired cashier, there is
opportunity to learn better loving. In more
significant relationships, it is vital to your
wellness that you acknowledge the rights of
the others to be just as they are and to sustain
them with your love and acceptance. Love
them unconditionally, while upholding and
attending to their most positive and healthy
behaviors. In the process, feel the letting go of
hurt and grudges, forgiving yourself as well.
Give yourself the same gifts of love and acceptance. Believe utterly in the never-ending
divinity of life expressed through us all.

Right now I feel in my heart the longing to give. I am deserving to be an instrument of giving.

The search is sweet for ones to receive your gifts right now. Feel no compulsion to give to all who need at once. Give of yourself where intuition guides, where the opportunity presents itself. You already know of the most inviting and pressing need, can feel the perfect way to give. You may sense that your health requires an outflowing now. Outpouring is wholesome, without need for gratitude or recognition. And, of course, we move gradually toward such purity, so go easy on yourself and love all your giving.

*I am tuned in to the infinite life force,
love force and capacity for good.*

There are glad surprises and numbers of blessings to be known. There are ways of gentleness and the joy of seeking the sacred light within each person you meet. There is the sparkle of the moonlight on snow and of sun on icicles in the morning. There is movement and music and muscle tone and laughter. And you are part of this vast and bountiful universe. You deserve it. We all do.

*I see myself reflected in
the natural world.*

As you watch rainbows run up and down spider webs in the early morning light, ponder what webs you are creating in your life. If you should accidentally walk through a web, be aware of the effects your actions have on many others. And consider the spider — how resilient and resourceful she is. She will build again and again. Notice the colors created by the web as the fibers act as prisms. How do you add color to your life? There is an infinity of natural metaphoric nourishment for creative and poetic understanding of yourself.

*I can choose to perceive a situation
differently, to create a new
interpretation of events.*

Black-or-white thinking is definitely dra-
matic yet not really supported in the natural
world. To best utilize the symbolism of
blackness, know that the state of black is in
one sense an absorption of all wavelengths of
light that we see as color. It could be said to
be holding the colors captive. You can release
them, the many other colors — the various
options and points of view. In white light is
the potential for all hues. Pass white light
through you, as if you were a living crystal
prism, and separate the colors. Consistently
brainstorm new ways to think about or
experience a situation. Acknowledge and let
go a vested interest in any one way. Limitation
is not possible. Enjoy making a rainbow of
your options.

NOVEMBER 18

*Money is a symbol of my honest offering
of good and helpful effort. The universe
supports this effort because it
flows from the heart.*

Your work is your life playing one of its
songs. However your giving is repaid, there is
an exchange of energy. There is a natural
rhythm to this exchange — an outpouring, an
inbringing, an offering, a gathering, a creating
and appreciating. The spirit of all this is
charged with your love, hopefully for the
work, essentially for yourself and for those
you serve.

I am at peace with my longing.

Your desires are a yeasting. You rise like fresh bread in the warmth of your cherished dreams. It is good to be quickened and increased by your wanting. You are alive! Use it in your favor — be real, yet even as you recognize illusions, love your longing.

NOVEMBER 20

I balance peaceful silence with free-flowing exchange.

Be comfortable in silence. Most people long for a listener. And in your silence be at rest. Watch your inner child need attention, approval. Watch your ego want power and recognition. Watch the nurturing parent part of you try to rescue others from the quiet. Give it all a rest. Take a deep breath and wait, relaxed. You will become wise and strong, you will learn and experience peace. When you speak, it will be an occasion of depth and honesty and delight.

*I protect my good feelings and intentions.
I surround them with a powerful force.*

Fashion a sanctuary for conditions of positive being. Words and images cast spells, so use them to champion your cause. Create a sphere of light, perhaps an image for your protection from inner or outer criticism. Surround yourself and breathe it in to strengthen your goodness and your Higher Self. Explore other images, sensations, affirmations. Your finest advocate is your abundant imagination.

*I can feel the exhilaration
of greater loving.*

Feelings of affection are wise forces. Left in freedom, without the inner censor, they flow straight from one heart to another. No matter who is with you or near you, when you choose to surrender judgment or expectation and simply love, there is joy. Focus on the one loved. Lose yourself in appreciation. No other communication is necessary for a higher energy to be known.

NOVEMBER 23

*I indulge myself with many constructive
behaviors and nurturing rewards.*

On behalf of yourself and our planet, know
that there is not enough time or life force for
us to indulge ourselves with negative
thoughts, attitudes or behaviors. It is important to watch for unhealthy behavior patterns
while unconditionally supporting your own
progress and well-being. Gradually add so
much good to your life that there is no room
left for negativity. Whatever is happening right
now, make the moment the best it can
possibly be. Indulge yourself well. And amply
reward the accomplishments with healthy
treats of limitless variety.

NOVEMBER 24

*I am patient with myself and
my progress.*

It has been said that to get from A to Z, most
of us have to go through G, M, P, Q and all the
other, sometimes mundane positions along
the way. Of course, you could win the lottery.
Meanwhile it is a wise choice to create your
own vision of Z, keep plotting the points and
moving along. Your particular movement is
unique to you, special and just right the way it
goes. That movement, of course, may include
some close road map examination and perhaps some changes, always with a benevolent
attitude. You really do deserve a gentle touch
along the way.

*I rise and rise into the realm
of extended joy.*

You can do it. You can expand those
periods of satisfaction or delight. It matters
not how often they occur. They do occur. And
it is the moment-to-moment creation and
extension of good feeling that creates fine
living, heroic being.

NOVEMBER 26

I exercise self-discipline in ways that increase my health and well-being.

From loving self-discipline comes the ultimate ability to regulate your life. If there is any real magic, it is surely to be found in the results of daily dedication to some freely chosen course of action, no matter how hard or boring or tedious it might become. You weigh it against the pay-offs and continue. You work the magic also in a situation that feels threatening, challenging or disappointing as you see yourself dealing with the issues, rather than suffering from or feeling victimized. You are a responsible person, able to accurately assess, accept and commit to positive action. You are the wizard in your own life's spell.

*I am transforming old thoughts and
perceptions of myself. I change it all
to compassion and unconditional love.*

It is time to transform the need to punish
yourself. You have suffered enough. You and
the others around you and our precious
planet deserve your light now. Give us all a
gift, the gift of your decision to transmute the
bitterness into a healing potion, in your own
good time. Use each old sad feeling or critical
thought as a signal to encourage, to fill your
cup with the milk of your own kindness.

*I often perceive the unfamiliar as
exciting and stimulating.*

Distress or worry may be familiar. You may
have a whole lifetime of coping behaviors
developed. Some of us find a comfort in
feeling right about a poor self-image. Comfort
and familiarity are largely over-rated, however.
Find some new pay-offs for conscious, step-
by-step creation of healthy, balanced, exciting
living. Gradually they become the only
rewards that count, and soon that life is its
own first prize.

NOVEMBER 29

*There is enough. I create space inside
to welcome ample health and all
manner of well-being.*

You are surrounded by plenty. There is
plenty of air; breathe it in. The breath is
healing; it is life. There is plenty of vital life
force. Release the blocks — the resentment,
the sadness, the tension. Express it, let it out,
share it with supportive people and allow the
space to increase for the infilling and expanding to happen. And there is enough to fill you.
There is enough forgiveness; give and receive
forgiveness. In consciousness forgive someone every hour if you need to, including
yourself. There is ample joy in simple things
like a bright red geranium or the smell of
warm bread. Abundance increases and ex-
tends into all life's nooks and corners. Be
ready now to receive and to give.

*I joyfully receive positive recognition
from others.*

You can remain humble and grateful to your many resources, even as you welcome compliments and other evidence that you are appreciated. You are becoming more skillful at recognizing such evidence, even if unspoken. And in the receiving, your well fills and spills over in your giving freely of recognition to others. So we increase, so we all bloom in all seasons.

DECEMBER 1

I am aware of the things I do well.
I use them to build my wholeness and
gather my goodness into strength.

Never negate that which comes easily for
you. It is a way that you channel and pass on
the miracles. Miraculous, too, is that which
comes hard to you yet which you value
enough to risk failure trying and which you
achieve, at whatever level, in whatever form,
even if different from your expectations.

DECEMBER 2

I am a being beyond measure. My boundless self emerges with unfolding wings.

Every daughter or son of the universe is created with immense potential. All of us share the same birthright, the right to question the limits. We often dwell inside walls we have helped to build. Start removing bricks. Try one small thing new today. Surprise yourself tomorrow. You have already begun.

DECEMBER 3

I am a whole person. I accept the
gifts of both male and female
qualities in myself.

Channels of ancient and enduring truths, many cultures share the concepts of *anima,* the female aspect within the man, and of *animus,* the male aspect of a woman. Native American belief holds that life itself is the child from the union of male and female elements of the universe, perceived as Mother Earth and Father Sky. The expansion of you beyond present boundaries and limitations can only be fully complete and satisfying if you validate both parts of your being. One will dominate and must be invited to allow the gifts of the other to be given and received. In the house of your whole self, encourage the full partnership of a sensitive nurturing strong man and a powerful loving woman.

DECEMBER 4

*I graciously accept areas of my adequacy,
of my higher abilities, as well as those
best left to others for now.*

It is all right to admit that something you
have tried to do or wanted to do is just not for
you right now. We do have to select a focus
for development and a primary outlet or two
for talent and energy. Evidence that you are
not particularly good at some things or
appreciated for them at any given time is
nothing to be ashamed of. Rather it is an
opportunity to let something go in order to
focus more intensely in another area of your
life or on another aspect of a situation.
Breathe spirit, breathe valor into your best
talents, however modest the beginning.
Celebrate some other folks in theirs. Allow
thoughts of praise to energize all the excellence we each can bring into the world.

DECEMBER 5

*I am increasingly comfortable
with intense feeling.*

You are sturdy and resilient. Honest strong feeling is no threat. You are not meant to be a guard at the door of emotion. Depth of caring sustains life. There is bound to be grief and love and all of the other magnificent expressions of our humanity that will ebb and flow forever in our lifetime. Sensitivity is desirable in both men and women. It is the mate of intensity. They are balanced by lightness and playfulness. All together they make us whole.

DECEMBER 6

I meet life as a sacred opportunity and
a gift. I respond fully with a
concentration of constructive energy.

Habitual anxiety blocks energy flow. Complaint and clinging sap creative juices. Be a noble warrior — concentrate your total attention on the campaign for constructive and creative living. If obstacles are perceived, do what is necessary and move ahead in grace and peace. Take however long it takes, one day at a time.

DECEMBER 7

*My life is unfolding in its own
way, its own time.*

There is peace in understanding that when
the time is right and you are ready, certain
things will fall into place. Something you
wanted terribly and forced may have been a
costly distraction. The coincidental occurren-
ces when timing feels perfect are no acci-
dents. They are part of our synchronous lives
— the meaningful meeting of self and opportunity in time and space. You are in charge of
continued and increasing readiness, awareness and courage.

*I give myself the time to create a healthy
and wonderful life. The process continues.
I am patient and persistent.*

Efficiency is to be congratulated, yet a
quality endeavor is not to be rushed. A life of
high awareness and healthy attitude is not a
hastily erected structure, but an infinite
dynamic happening. There is always more, so
relax into it and feel the glory of how far you
have come. Set your impatience out of yourself. Listen to your urgency and then transform
it to liveliness, so vitality can flow unrestrict-
ed. Remember every moment your universal
purpose and the sacredness of your journey.

*I reach out to others in loving ways,
no matter what.*

We cannot only be loving when we feel good, when we are less busy, when the bills are all paid, the house is clean, when feeling high self-esteem, when certain people love us back, when only certain kinds of people are around . . . We are to be congratulated when we act in loving ways as consistently as possible, no matter who, no matter what, even when we do not really feel like it. At precisely those times, we are taking the opportunity to truly love unselfishly and unconditionally. At those times we are heroic.

I am grateful to these winter days for the gifts only this season can bring.

There are bare skeletons of trees that reveal an intricate sky pattern. In late afternoon, sun may transform the limbs to gold. Notice the space between the branches and how the space is at least half the form. On days of cloud, you may be blessed with a subtle pearliness at sunrise — a quiet loveliness, a peace. Bring this into your being. Stop on clear mornings to breathe the crispness, feel the awakening, see the light softly filtered through misty breath of rising day. In the evening there may be flocks of wintering birds energizing the sky. Listen; receive the vital force. Allow purification from the wind. And in the cozy inside hours, pamper yourself, rest, renew. Be one with the rhythm of the seasons and know that in the winter of your years your gathering wisdom will be offered and in this will be great joy.

*I am happy to promote creative,
cooperative decision-making
and problem-solving.*

Creativity is so much more than the fine arts. Actually all creativity is a fine art, the art of remaining open to options, accessible to inspiration, free to explore without defending old, well-trodden territory. When others are involved in decisions with you, rise to the occasion with fresh loving tolerance of all ideas. Allow your innocent self to be excited at the unlimited possibilities of synergistic problem-solving. You cannot yet imagine what may result when two or more creators actually become more than the sum of their parts.

I am mellow and flexible, and I focus on loving the people this holiday season.

You know exactly what is most important, and it is not hurrying from one shop to another, buying what you "should" and possibly cannot afford. This often leaves you drained and impatient, frustrated. You are aware more than ever before how vital is the touch, the long look of appreciation square in the eyes, the time to be together sharing the pieces of your lives. This special season offers us all the chance to live according to our most noble values. It is a time to honor people with acts of love. You are more capable now of finding the balance and being comfortable there. This is your gift to yourself — this participation in the birth of true giving.

I feel the quiet in a deep inner space.
I go there often to find strength.

Go to the home of your Wise Self, breathe there, focus there. Feel the hassles, anxiety and bad feelings melt away and be in touch with gentle power. Enjoy the sensation of groundedness and holiness; anticipate profound understanding. Expect nothing, however. Simply be present and welcome what comes.

*I focus on what is in my best interest,
on what is working in my life, on what
keeps my face turned toward the light.*

Know that you can live up to only one set of
standards at a time — the set you actively
create for yourself, based on actual outcomes
and feelings. Let the notions of normal or
perfect or ideal go. Give your full energy to
noticing and strengthening whatever seems to
result in long-term satisfaction, intimacy,
health, joy, productivity and other solid pay-
offs. Trust your maturing sense of what is right
for you.

It is perfectly okay to admit, "I don't know," and to seek help in finding answers and understanding.

All of us have areas of solid strength and areas where we may need to fill in some spaces. Often when we admit to needing the benefit of another pilgrim's knowledge, wisdom or experience, we encourage others to take risks in finding help along the way. Discomfort in this process is temporary. The gain may be immeasurable, including enriched relationships.

I laugh often and heartily.
My laughter is good medicine.

Our laughter is a special tonic sending out endorphins, the body's natural chemicals, to relieve pain and tension. Laughter ripples deliciously over sore backs and hurt feelings. Laughter and fun stimulate the immune system. Nothing else quite measures up to a full dose of mirth, provided it is not at anyone's expense, given that there is only nurture intended. Be happy — giggle, guffaw, chuckle and roar. Set it up for yourself. Go on — get tickled!

DECEMBER 17

*I am courageous and enthusiastic as
I seek to be shown how I can
best be of service.*

Our lives are organic, ever-changing. We
continually seek the revelation of the finest
and most fulfilling avenue for giving to our
world. A voice or feeling deep inside will help
you, if you are patient and listen bravely. Your
present way may be validated or questioned.
Be willing to search or flow with the dynamic,
living force that motivates your most vital
giving.

DECEMBER 18

*I am ready for fullness of life and
for limitless opportunity.*

Send out a bulletin to your subconscious —
the self-imposed or out-grown boundaries are
no longer accepted. The limitations are
recognized as illusions and are melting away.
You will begin to tune in to more each day.
Each challenge or conflict will be a teacher.
Every person will be an opening to a new
universe of perception and experience. Every
day will open with an affirmation of gratitude
for so being — in readiness for more in all
dimensions. It is sure to come if so strongly
invited.

DECEMBER 19

I know that I can change only myself
and my responses. I am invitational
and respectful of differences when
I do offer my influence.

Graciously acknowledge that you are responsible for your reactions, not for the behavior of others. It is highly enlightening to watch yourself in an uncomfortable situation, as an interested observer, not as a judge. Notice whether you are possibly over-reacting, behaving according to your personal values, adding any positive or negative material. Relax and allow your wise, intuitive self to direct the most accepting attitude and most helpful action.

*I am adept at wisely sharing my
personal self, my experience,
my inner life.*

You move surely in the direction of a more
excellent balance between withholding intimacy and over-abundant transparency. If you
feel like you are holding back when sharing at
a deeper personal level might facilitate
closeness or be helpful to others, simply
begin to watch yourself kindly, learning your
patterns and motivations. You are much less
vulnerable than you might think and have
plenty of ego-strength to begin to bring this
part of your life into better balance. Whatever
you might be restraining or think you are
concealing is known already at some level.
The question is whether the sharing would be
self-indulgent or potentially honest, equal
communication of shared humanity.

I generously share the gifts of growth and understanding that I have gained.

The Native American Indian concept of the "give-away" is a loving and effective way of allowing positive universal energy to flow through you, through your caring heart and out into the world. As you learn more and more to see negativity as grist for the mill, as you learn how to transform more fully challenges into changes, it will be natural to practice the "give-away" path. You will know when to hold and nurture what you have learned and when you are ready to share with confidence and humility. You will know. We are all wonderful teachers of one another and have much of value to give in our own time.

*This season I create extraordinary
meaning from ordinary moments.
Glory shines in unexpected places.*

Perhaps your holiday spirit is more uplifted by a special moment with a child than by a fancy party or expensive gifts. It may be that joking and hugging in the kitchen while helping a friend bake cookies is what the season is all about for you. It could be that the smell of wood chips, hearty laughter or communion with nature make the gathering for yule fires a festival in itself. Let a crisp, star-filled night fill your heart with wonder. Shine that wonder out everywhere and miss none of the unanticipated gifts that mean so much. You are worth it.

*I am awake and aware of life options
and resources in variety and abundance.
I am a powerful force in my
own enriched life.*

We must continuously be aware of the situations where we have choices and protect ourselves from power-leakage. Institutions and out-moded or ill-founded cultural patterns can rob us of our birthright of choice and the excitement of exploration and creation. Begin to reclaim your power, for example, as you decide what is an appropriate level of consumerism at holiday times. Invent new customs with family and friends around giving. Co-create fresh rituals and celebrations that are more personally meaningful to you and the others. In these ways you are a talented artist, capable and committed to making a more beautiful life.

DECEMBER 24

*I find and create meaningful ritual and
joyful celebration to facilitate
connection among the people I love.*

We are strong enough to challenge
consumerism, hurried socializing and the
tension it all perpetuates. A beautiful alterna-
tive involves the discovery of ceremony and
traditional activities that are thoughtfully
selected and cooperatively enlivened with
many creative ideas. Winter solstice rituals, for
example, tune us in and help us know the
mystery and majesty of natural cycles and
feelings of unity with all people out of all time
and space who have celebrated the earth
heritage in the ancient ways, adapted to
present needs. A rich body of old and new
tradition is waiting to be discovered and
made-to-order for families and extended
families. Such sharing will bring much love
and deep meaning to the holidays.

DECEMBER 25

*I send a prayer to a brilliant star and
I know it is shining on a friend
far away. A strong blessing returns.*

On Christmas Day indulge in some creative communication with the stars, the moon, a planet and a friend. Imagine how the light that graces yourself shines at the same moment on someone in a distant place. Send your gift of some good energy, some courage, a prayer to that heavenly object to be beamed to the one far away. Be in tune with the power in our solar system, our galaxy — the worlds among worlds among worlds. Link this world and another with a wish for a fellow traveller. Send good things to anyone, anything, anywhere, especially where there is a need for encouragement or healing. Be ready to be enriched far beyond the giving.

*I have a knowing deep inside.
I am still, focusing on my
inner sense of the issue.*

Pay attention to your breath, simply following it as it enters your nostrils, flows deep and
exits. Relax and be calm. Ask yourself what is
between you and full well-being. Feel the
answer in your body. What is your sense of it?
Wait and patiently listen to your body wisdom. How does it feel in your body? What
does it need? Receive the knowing and feel
for more. Allow yourself to put any remaining
discomfort outside your body for as long as
you need. See what you learn from your inner
wisdom, your mind-body team.

*I love and accept others right now,
just the way they are.*

Only when we surrender the conditions for loving can we begin to participate respectfully in a shared growth adventure. If we feel superior or mask feelings of inferiority with one-up behavior, the circuits of exchange are shorted-out. Almost always, the unconditional love and support are plenty to offer another. Occasionally your instincts may guide you to offer more. Be ready to listen, keep listening, touch base with the loving, listen more. Remain patient, wholly present and un-attached to outcomes, unless the behavior threatens your well-being. Be ready to recognize successes, however modest. And trust in the rightness of the progress and the path of the other, at whatever pace, on whatever plane. It is their journey and it is an honor to participate.

*My attention is a magnet, attracting what
I want to have in my life.*

Recognize that what is energized with your
consistent attention has the greatest potential
for becoming a major part of your reality. If
you wish beauty to become more a part of
your life experience, yet you focus mainly on
the growing litter problem and become
depressed at urban unsightliness, there will
be little energy for the attraction and addition
of beauty. By all means, notice what needs to
be done and make a choice as to what you
will do, meanwhile staying tuned eagerly to
the good. Thus the world becomes a mirror
for your highest expectations; soon there will
cease to be a division between yourself and
the best that the universe has to offer.

DECEMBER 29

*I unconditionally claim a good
feeling, a happy time.*

Let pure good moments shine. Experience
them completely, regardless of external pre-
or post-conditions that may or may not be
realized. Place no prerequisites or future
qualifiers on good feeling. Be with it in the
present. Whether or not the price is right, love
that dream house now. Let the excitement
quicken you. Even if the magazine article
might not sell, celebrate that joyous high
when you finish it. Even as the rain clouds
gather, soak up the sun shining in the present
moment. You will have more energy to do
something wonderful in the rain.

*I move in harmony with the cycles,
circles, seasons of my life.*

There is a season for dropping old foliage, for dormancy, for renewal, for rapid change and growth. Know that nothing is permanent; there is always progress in a cycle that follows natural rhythms. Do not fear or hold tight to a phase. You change just as the moon does, as the year's passing, as the wild herd's numbers rise and fall, as the waters ebb and flow. You, too, are a circling world, yet unique in that you spiral upward with each round.

DECEMBER 31

I have seen the rainbow.
I carry it within me.

Take hold of the perfection, the peak moments, the joy, the love that has been given you. Know that they all live within; they are always there for you. They accumulate; with awareness and gratitude, they grow in power and they never end.

Best Sellers From HCI

ISBN	TITLE	PRICE
0-932194-15-X	Adult Children of Alcoholics	$6.95
0-932194-54-0	Bradshaw On: The Family	$9.95
0-932194-26-5	Choicemaking	$9.95
0-932194-21-4	Co-Dependency	$6.95
0-932194-61-3	Following The Yellow Brick Road	$9.95
0-932194-40-0	Healing The Child Within	$8.95
0-932194-39-7	Learning To Love Yourself	$7.95
0-932194-25-7	Struggle For Intimacy	$6.95
0-932194-68-0	Twelve Steps To Self-Parenting For Adult Children	$7.95

Orders must be prepaid by check, money order, MasterCard or Visa. Purchase orders from agencies accepted (attach P.O. documentation) for billing. Net 30 days.

Minimum shipping/handling — $1.25 for orders less than $25. For orders over $25, add 5% of total for shipping and handling. Florida residents add 6% sales tax.

Health Communications, Inc.
Enterprise Center, 3201 S.W. 15th Street
Deerfield Beach, FL 33442
(800) 851-9100

More Affirmation Books

DAILY AFFIRMATIONS: For Adult Children of Alcoholics
Rokelle Lerner

Affirmations are positive, powerful statements that will change the ways we think, feel and behave. *Daily Affirmations* has also been recorded on audiocassette, where author Lerner is joined by Dr. Joseph Cruse.

ISBN 0-932194-27-3 .... $ 6.95

Set of Six 90-Minute Tapes
ISBN 0-932194-49-4 .... $39.95

SAY YES TO LIFE: Daily Meditations for Recovery
Leo Booth

Say Yes To Life takes you through the year day by day looking for answers and sometimes discovering that there are none. Father Leo tells us, "For the recovering compulsive person God is too important to miss — may you find Him now."

ISBN 0-932194-46-X .... $ 6.95

TIME FOR JOY
Ruth Fishel

With delightful illustrations by Bonny Lowell, Ruth Fishel takes you gently through the year, affirming that wherever you are today is perfect and now is the *TIME FOR JOY!*

ISBN 0-932194-82-6 .... $6.95